KITCHEN
TABLE

100 Easy Chinese Suppers
KEN HOM

www.mykitchentable.co.uk

Welcome to my KITCHEN TABLE

Cooking Chinese food doesn't have to be difficult – many of our long-held culinary traditions lend themselves to **simple and effortless meals** that taste fresh, light and packed with delectable flavours.

Contents

Classic Chinese Chicken Stock

Your first step on the path to success with Chinese cooking is to prepare and maintain an ample supply of good chicken stock. I prefer to make a large amount and freeze it. Once you have a batch of stock available you will be able to prepare any number of soups or sauces very quickly.

Step one Put all the chicken into a very large pot (the bones can be put in either frozen or defrosted). Cover with the cold water and bring to a simmer.

Step two Using a large, shallow spoon, skim off the scum as it rises from the bones to the surface of the water. Watch the heat, as the stock should never boil. Keep skimming as necessary until the stock looks clear. This can take 20–40 minutes at a low simmer. Do not stir or disturb the stock.

Step three Now add the ginger, spring onions, garlic cloves and salt. Simmer the stock over a very low heat for 2–4 hours, skimming any fat off the top at least twice. The stock should be rich and full-bodied, which is why it needs to be simmered for such a long time.

Step four Strain the stock through several layers of dampened muslin or through a very fine sieve. Let it cool thoroughly, then chill. Remove any fat that has risen to the top. It is now ready to be used or transferred to containers and frozen for future use.

Makes 5 litres (8 pints)

2kg (4½ lb) raw chicken feet, wings, etc., or any leftover bones you may have (save uncooked chicken bones and keep them in the freezer until you need them)

675g (1½ lb) chicken pieces, such as wings, thighs, drumsticks

5 litres (8 pints) cold water

3 slices fresh root ginger, cut on the diagonal into 5 x 1cm (2 x ½ in) slices

6 spring onions, green tops removed

6 garlic cloves, unpeeled, but lightly crushed

1 tsp salt

Vietnamese Beef and Spinach Soup

This Vietnamese soup is similar to one I grew up with in our Chinese household. We used a variety of water spinach with a crisp stalk and distinctive flavour. I have found, however, that ordinary spinach works just as well. This light soup is typical of the subtle cuisine of Vietnam. It is easy to make, and much of the preparation can be done in advance.

Serves 4

450g (1lb) fresh spinach

175g (6oz) lean fillet steak, cut into thin slices about 5cm (2in) long

2 shallots, finely sliced

2 tbsp finely chopped garlic

3 tbsp fish sauce (nam pla)

1.2 litres (2 pints) home-made chicken stock (see page 7) or good-quality bought stock

1 tbsp lemon juice

1 tsp sugar

1 small fresh red chilli, de-seeded and chopped

freshly ground black pepper

Step one Remove the stalks from the spinach and wash the leaves well. Blanch the leaves for a few seconds in a large pan of boiling water until they are just wilted. Then drain well and refresh in cold water to prevent further cooking. Drain again, squeezing out excess water.

Step two Combine the slices of steak with the shallots, garlic, 1 tablespoon of the fish sauce and some freshly ground black pepper, then set aside. (The soup can be prepared in advance up to this point.)

Step three Just before you are ready to eat, bring the chicken stock to a simmer in a saucepan and season it with the remaining fish sauce, the lemon juice, sugar and chilli.

Step four Add the blanched spinach and stir in the beef and its marinade. Bring the soup back to simmering point, add a few grindings of freshly ground black pepper to taste and serve at once.

Have you made this recipe? Tell us what you think at
www.mykitchentable.co.uk/blog

KITCHEN
TABLE

Vietnamese Soup with Beancurd

This hearty, colourful soup is light and healthy, yet is almost a meal in itself. I am reminded how similar it is to many of the soups from southern China. Easy to make, it relies on good chicken stock for its success.

Step one In a bowl, combine the pork, prawns, 2 teaspoons of the fish sauce and the spring onions. Leave to marinate for about 10 minutes.

Step two Gently cut the beancurd into 1cm (½in) cubes and leave to drain on kitchen paper for 10 minutes.

Step three Pour the chicken stock into a saucepan and bring to a simmer. Add the marinated prawn and pork mixture and simmer for 2 minutes.

Step four Add the beancurd and the remaining fish sauce and simmer for another 2 minutes. Season to taste with salt and pepper, then remove from the heat, garnish with the chives and chillies and serve.

Serves 4

100g (4oz) lean, boneless pork chops, cut into thin slices 5cm (2in) long

100g (4oz) raw prawns, shelled and de-veined, tails on

5 tsp fish sauce (nam pla)

2 tbsp chopped spring onions (white part only)

450g (1lb) silken or firm beancurd

1.2 litres (2 pints) home-made chicken stock (see page 7) or good-quality bought stock

salt and freshly ground black pepper

to garnish

3 tbsp chopped fresh chives

2 fresh red chillies, de-seeded and chopped

Indonesian-style Chicken Soup

Many years ago, when I was in Jakarta, a brilliant cook hosted a wonderful buffet consisting of all the regional dishes of Indonesia. This spicy soup was one of my favourites. It relies on really good chicken stock for its success, and makes a zesty starter for any meal.

Serves 4

100g (4oz) fresh or dried egg noodles

1 tsp sesame oil

3 tbsp groundnut oil

6 garlic cloves, finely sliced

6 shallots, finely sliced

2 tsp shrimp paste

1 tsp ground turmeric

1 tbsp ground coriander

2 tsp ground cumin

2 tsp salt

2 fresh red or green chillies, de-seeded and finely shredded

1.2 litres (2 pints) home-made chicken stock (see page 7) or good-quality bought stock

2 tsp lemon juice

freshly ground black pepper

to garnish

2 spring onions, finely shredded

2 eggs, hard-boiled for 10 minutes, then shelled and quartered

prawn crackers

1 lime, cut into wedges

Step one Cook the noodles for 3–5 minutes in a pan of boiling water until tender. Drain and plunge them into cold water. Drain again thoroughly and toss them with the sesame oil, then set aside.

Step two Heat a wok or large frying pan over a high heat. Add the groundnut oil and, when it is very hot and slightly smoking, add the garlic and shallots. Stir-fry them until they are crisp and golden brown. Remove with a slotted spoon, drain on kitchen paper and set aside.

Step three Now add the shrimp paste, turmeric, coriander, cumin, salt, chillies and some freshly ground black pepper to the wok and stir-fry for 1 minute.

Step four Add the stock, turn the heat to low, then cover and simmer for 10 minutes. Stir in the lemon juice and simmer for another 2 minutes. Ladle into a large soup tureen, add the cooked noodles and serve at once with the garnishes, including the fried garlic and shallots, in separate bowls.

Savoury Rice Soup

This is the Thai version of a gentle rice soup that can be found throughout Asia. The Chinese make it thick and creamy whereas *kao tom*, as it is known in Thailand, is more of a thin broth. However it is made, it is true comfort food, savoury and nurturing. Feel free to add your favourite cooked meat, poultry or seafood, or just serve it simply, with garnishes such as the ones listed below.

Step one Combine the cooked rice and stock in a large saucepan and bring to a simmer. Add the fish sauce and black pepper and simmer for 5 minutes.

Step two Heat a wok or large frying pan over a medium heat. Add the oil and, when it is hot, stir in the garlic. Reduce the heat and stir-fry gently for 20 seconds, until the garlic is lightly browned. Remove and drain on kitchen paper.

Step three Pour the rice and stock into the wok and simmer for 2 minutes. Turn into a soup tureen and serve at once with the garnishes, including the fried garlic.

Serves 2–4

100g (4oz) cooked long-grain white rice

1.2 litres (2 pints) home-made chicken stock (see page 7) or good-quality bought stock

3 tbsp fish sauce (nam pla)

1½ tbsp vegetable oil

3 tbsp finely chopped garlic

freshly ground black pepper to taste

to garnish

2 spring onions, finely shredded

1 tbsp finely shredded fresh root ginger

1–2 small fresh red or green Thai chillies, de-seeded and finely shredded

a handful of fresh coriander leaves

15

Coconut Chicken Soup

No mistaking the Thai heritage here: coconut is a marker of authentic Thai cuisine. This soup, called *tom kha gai*, has a richness one associates with cream, but in fact, it is due to the coconut milk, the opulence and aroma of which add so much to the dish, making it almost a meal in itself.

Serves 4

2 fresh sticks of lemon grass

1.5 litres (2½ pints) home-made chicken stock (see page 7) or good-quality bought stock

2 tbsp coarsely chopped fresh galangal or root ginger

6 kaffir lime leaves, or 2 tbsp coarsely chopped lime zest

6 tbsp finely sliced shallots

225g (8oz) skinless, boneless chicken thighs

3 tbsp fish sauce (nam pla)

4 tbsp lime juice

2 fresh red or green Thai chillies, de-seeded and finely shredded

1 tbsp sugar

1 x 400ml (14fl oz) tin coconut milk

a handful of fresh Thai basil leaves or ordinary basil leaves, to garnish

Step one Peel off the tough outer layers of the lemon grass sticks, leaving the tender whitish centre. Cut it into 7.5cm (3in) pieces and crush with the flat of a heavy knife.

Step two Put the stock in a large saucepan with the lemon grass, galangal or ginger, lime leaves or zest and half the shallots. Bring to the boil, then reduce the heat, cover and simmer gently for 1 hour. Strain through a sieve, discarding the lemon grass, galangal, lime and shallots, then return the stock to the pan.

Step three Cut the chicken into 2.5cm (1in) chunks and add to the strained stock, together with the fish sauce, lime juice, chillies, sugar, coconut milk and the remaining shallots. Bring to the boil, then reduce the heat and simmer for 8 minutes. Transfer the soup to a large tureen, garnish with the basil leaves and serve at once.

KITCHEN TABLE

For more recipes from My Kitchen Table, sign up for our newsletter at www.mykitchentable.co.uk/newsletter

Crispy 'Seaweed'

This is one of the most popular Chinese restaurant dishes in the West. A special type of seaweed is used in China, but it is not yet available elsewhere, so Chinese cabbage is used instead. This is a good example of the adaptability of Chinese cuisine: if the original ingredients are not available, technique and ingenuity will overcome the deficiency. This dish is delicious and easy to make, and, speaking of adaptability, can also be tried with fresh spinach leaves.

Step one Separate the stalks from the stem of the pak choy and then cut the green leaves from the white stalks. (Save the stalks; you can stir-fry them with garlic or use them for soup.)

Step two Wash the leaves in several changes of cold water, then drain them thoroughly and dry in a salad spinner. Roll the leaves up tightly, a few at a time, and finely shred them into strips 5mm (¼ in) wide.

Step three Preheat the oven to 120°C/250°F/gas ½. Spread the cabbage strips out on a baking sheet and put in the preheated oven for 15 minutes to dry slightly. They should not be completely dry or they will burn when fried. Remove from the oven and leave to cool. This can be done the day before.

Step four Heat a wok over a high heat, then add the oil. When the oil is hot and slightly smoking, deep-fry the greens in 3 or 4 batches. After about 30–40 seconds, when they turn crisp and green, remove them immediately from the wok and drain well on kitchen paper. Leave to cool.

Step five Toss the crispy greens with the salt and sugar. Garnish with the pine nuts and serve.

Serves 4

1.25kg (2½ lb) pak choy (Chinese white cabbage)

900ml (1½ pints) groundnut oil

1 tsp salt

2 tsp sugar

50g (2oz) pine nuts, lightly roasted

Crispy Fried Wontons

Wontons make a great snack or a tasty starter for any meal.

Serves 6

225g (8oz) wonton skins, thawed if necessary

600ml (1 pint) groundnut or vegetable oil

for the filling

350g (12oz) raw prawns, shelled, de-veined and coarsely minced or chopped

100g (4oz) minced fatty pork

2 tsp salt

½ tsp freshly ground black pepper

4 tbsp finely chopped spring onions

2 tsp finely chopped fresh root ginger

2 tsp Shaoxing rice wine or dry sherry

1 tsp sugar

2 tsp sesame oil

1 egg white, beaten

for the dipping sauce

2 tbsp sugar

3 tbsp Chinese white rice vinegar or cider vinegar

3 tbsp tomato paste or tomato ketchup

1 tsp salt

¼ tsp freshly ground white pepper

1 tsp cornflour

Step one For the filling, put the prawns and pork in a bowl, add the salt and pepper and mix well, either by kneading with your hand or stirring with a wooden spoon. Add all the remaining filling ingredients and stir well. Cover with clingfilm and chill for at least 20 minutes.

Step two In a small saucepan, combine all the ingredients for the dipping sauce except the cornflour with 150ml (¼ pint) water and bring to the boil. Blend the cornflour with 2 teaspoons water and stir this mixture into the pan. Cook for 1 minute, then remove from the heat and leave to cool.

Step three To stuff the wontons, put 1 tablespoon of the filling in the centre of each skin. Dampen the edges with a little water and bring them up around the filling. Pinch together at the top, so that the wonton is sealed; it should look like a small, filled bag.

Step four Heat a wok or large frying pan over a high heat. Add the oil and, when it is very hot and slightly smoking, deep-fry the wontons, a handful at a time, for 2–3 minutes or until golden and crisp. If they brown too quickly, reduce the heat slightly. Drain the wontons well on kitchen paper, then serve immediately with the sweet and sour dipping sauce.

Crispy Corn Cakes

These make a wonderfully enticing starter – a savoury mixture of corn and pork fried to crispy morsels. Serve them with sweet chilli dipping sauce (see page 24). Their Thai name is *tod mun khao phod*.

Step one If using corn on the cob, strip off the husks and the silk and cut off the kernels with a sharp knife or cleaver. You should end up with about 275g (10oz). If you are using tinned corn, drain it well.

Step two Put half the corn in a blender, add all the remaining ingredients except the oil and blend to a purée. Pour this mixture into a bowl and stir in the rest of the corn.

Step three Heat a wok or large frying pan over a high heat. Add the oil and, when it is very hot and slightly smoking, pour in a small ladleful of the corn mixture. Repeat until the wok is full. Reduce the heat to low and cook for 1–2 minutes, until the fritters are brown underneath, then turn them over and fry the other side.

Step four Remove the fritters from the wok with a slotted spoon and drain on kitchen paper. Keep them warm while you cook the remaining fritters. Arrange on a warm platter, garnish with the coriander and sliced cucumber and serve at once.

Serves 4–6

450g (1lb) corn on the cob, or 275g (10oz) tinned sweetcorn

175g (6oz) minced fatty pork

2 tbsp finely chopped fresh coriander

2 tbsp finely chopped garlic

2 tbsp fish sauce (nam pla)

½ tsp freshly ground white pepper

1 tsp sugar

1 tbsp cornflour

2 eggs, beaten

600ml (1 pint) vegetable oil, for deep-frying

to garnish

a handful of fresh coriander sprigs

1 small cucumber, peeled and thinly sliced

Crispy Wontons with Sweet Chilli Sauce

These Thai-style wontons can be kept in the fridge for up to a week.

Serves 6

225g (8oz) wonton skins, thawed if necessary

600ml (1 pint) vegetable oil, for deep-frying

for the dipping sauce

175g (6oz) large red chillies, finely chopped

3 tbsp chopped garlic

1 tbsp sugar

1 tbsp white rice vinegar or malt vinegar

1 tbsp fish sauce (nam pla)

1 tbsp vegetable oil

salt to taste

for the filling

100g (4oz) raw prawns, shelled, de-veined and coarsely chopped

350g (12oz) minced fatty pork

2 tsp salt

1 tsp freshly ground black pepper

2 tbsp finely chopped garlic

3 tbsp finely chopped spring onions

2 tbsp fish sauce (nam pla)

1 tsp sugar

3 tbsp finely chopped fresh coriander

1 egg, lightly beaten

Step one Put all the ingredients for the sweet chilli sauce in a wok or saucepan with 150ml (¼ pint) water and bring to the boil. Reduce the heat to very low, cover and simmer gently for 15 minutes. Remove from the heat and leave to cool.

Step two Purée the mixture in a blender or food-processor until it is a smooth paste. Reheat in a wok or saucepan for about 3 minutes to bring out the flavour, adding more salt if necessary. Once cool, it is ready to use or can be stored in the fridge.

Step three Next make the filling for the wontons. Put the prawns and pork in a large bowl, add the salt and pepper and mix well, either by kneading with your hand or by stirring with a wooden spoon. Add the rest of the filling ingredients and stir them well into the prawn and pork mixture. Cover with clingfilm and chill for at least 20 minutes.

Step four To stuff the wontons, put about a tablespoon of the filling in the centre of each wonton skin. Dampen the edges with a little water and bring them up around the filling. Pinch the edges together at the top, so that the wonton is sealed; it should look like a small, filled bag.

Step five Heat a wok or large frying pan over a high heat and add the oil. When it is hot, add a handful of wontons and deep-fry for 3 minutes, until golden and crisp. (If they turn brown too quickly, reduce the heat slightly.) Drain well on kitchen paper and then fry the remaining wontons. Serve immediately, with the sweet chilli dipping sauce.

Vietnamese Prawn Paste Skewers

This delightful appetiser is known in Vietnamese as *chao tom*. It can be made well in advance and grilled at the last moment, making it an ideal starter as well as a very original one.

Step one For the paste, using a cleaver or a large, sharp knife, chop the prawns coarsely and then mince them finely into a paste. Transfer to a bowl and mix in the rest of the ingredients for the prawn paste, adding a little more cornflour if the mixture is too moist (alternatively, you could do all this in a food-processor). This step can be done several hours in advance, but you should then wrap the paste well in clingfilm and put it in the fridge until you need it.

Step two Lightly oil your hands with sesame oil. Take about 2 tablespoons of the prawn paste and wrap it evenly around a length of sugar cane, leaving about 1cm (½in) exposed at each end. Repeat with the remaining prawn paste and sugar cane. You should have around 10 pieces.

Step three Set up a steamer, or put a rack into a wok or deep saucepan and fill it with 5cm (2in) of water. Bring the water to the boil over a high heat. Put the prawn pieces on a heatproof plate and then carefully lower it into the steamer or on to the rack. Reduce the heat to low and cover the wok or pan tightly. Steam gently for 3 minutes. The prawn skewers can be made in advance up to this point.

Step four When you are ready to serve the skewers, prepare a barbecue or preheat a ridged chargrill pan or the oven grill. When the charcoal is ash white or the grill is very hot, grill the prawns for 3 minutes on each side. Put the cooked skewers on a warm platter and serve immediately. To eat, remove the prawn paste from the cane, wrap in a lettuce leaf with a few sprigs of herbs and dip into the sauce. Of course, one can always chew on the sugar cane.

Serves 4

sesame oil

1 or 2 pieces fresh sugar cane, cut into about ten 7.5cm (3in) lengths

225g (8oz) iceberg lettuce, leaves separated

assorted fresh basil, mint or coriander sprigs, or all 3

1 quantity of Dipping Sauce (see page 31)

for the prawn paste

450g (1lb) raw prawns, shelled and de-veined

100g (4oz) minced fatty pork

1 tsp salt

½ tsp freshly ground black pepper

1 egg white

2 tbsp finely chopped spring onions (white part only)

2 tbsp finely chopped garlic

1 tsp finely chopped fresh ginger

1 tsp cornflour (more if needed)

2 tsp sugar

1 tsp fish sauce (nam pla)

Spring Rolls

Serve these spring rolls with the Sweet and Sour Dipping Sauce on page 24.

Makes about 15–18

1 packet spring
roll skins

1 egg, beaten

1.2 litres (2 pints)
groundnut oil

for the filling

25g (1oz) dried Chinese
black mushrooms

100g (4oz) raw prawns,
shelled, de-veined and
very finely chopped

100g (4oz) minced
fatty pork

1½ tbsp groundnut oil

2 tbsp chopped garlic

1 tbsp finely chopped
fresh root ginger

1½ tbsp light soy sauce

1 tbsp Shaoxing rice
wine or dry sherry

3 tbsp finely chopped
spring onions

1 tsp salt

½ tsp freshly ground
black pepper

225g (8oz) Chinese
leaves, finely shredded

for the marinade

1 tsp light soy sauce

1 tsp Shaoxing rice
wine or dry sherry

1 tsp sesame oil

½ tsp salt

½ tsp freshly ground
black pepper

Step one Soak the dried mushrooms in warm water, then drain and thoroughly dry them. Remove and discard the stems and finely shred the mushrooms.

Step two Combine the prawns and pork with all the marinade ingredients in a small bowl.

Step three Heat a wok over a high heat. Add the 1½ tablespoons of groundnut oil and, when it is very hot and slightly smoking, add the garlic and ginger and stir-fry for 20 seconds.

Step four Add all the rest of the filling ingredients, including the mushrooms and the prawn and meat mixture, and stir-fry for 5 minutes. Place the mixture in a colander to drain and leave to cool thoroughly.

Step five Place 3–4 tablespoons of the filling near the end of each spring roll skin, then fold in the sides and roll up tightly.

Step six Seal the open end by brushing a small amount of the beaten egg along the edge, then pressing together gently. You should have a roll about 10cm (4in) long, a little like an oversized cigar.

Step seven Rinse out the wok and reheat it over a high heat, then add the oil for deep-frying. When the oil is hot and slightly smoking, gently drop in as many spring rolls as will fit easily in one layer. Fry the spring rolls until golden brown and cooked through, about 4 minutes. Adjust the heat as necessary. Remove with a slotted spoon, drain on a wire rack, then on kitchen paper. Cook the remaining spring rolls in the same way. Serve them at once, hot and crispy, with the sweet and sour sauce for dipping.

Crispy Vietnamese Spring Rolls

This is perhaps one of the tastiest versions of spring rolls in all of Asia.

Step one For the filling, soak the noodles in a large bowl of warm water for 15 minutes. When soft, drain them and cut into 7.5cm (3in) lengths, using scissors or a knife. Finely chop the onion.

Step two Soak the Chinese mushrooms in warm water for about 20 minutes, until soft. Rinse in cold water and squeeze dry. Remove any hard stalks and finely shred the mushrooms.

Step three Meanwhile, make the dipping sauce. De-seed and chop the chillies and combine with all the other ingredients in a blender along with 4 tablespoons water, processing thoroughly. Pour into a small bowl and leave to stand for at least 10 minutes.

Step four Heat a wok or large frying pan over a high heat. Add the groundnut oil for the filling and, when it is very hot, add the onion, garlic, spring onions and shallots and stir-fry for 3 minutes. Add the pork and salt and pepper and continue to stir-fry for 5 minutes. Drain in a colander and leave to cool.

Step five Combine the cooled mixture in a large bowl with the bean-thread noodles, mushrooms and crab meat.

Step six To make the spring rolls, fill a large bowl with warm water. Dip a rice paper wrapper in the water and let it soften, then remove and drain on a tea-towel. Repeat with the rest. Transfer the wrappers to a board, put about 2 tablespoons of the filling on each, then fold in each side and roll up tightly.

Step seven Heat the oil in a deep-fat fryer or a large wok. Deep-fry the spring rolls until they are golden brown. They have a tendency to stick to each other, so fry only a few at a time. Do not attempt to break them apart should they stick together – do this after they have been removed from the oil. Drain on kitchen paper and serve with the lettuce, herb sprigs and dipping sauce.

Makes about 25

1 packet 15cm (6in) round rice paper wrappers

5 tbsp plain flour, mixed with 6 tbsp cold water

400ml (14fl oz) oil, preferably groundnut

225g (8oz) iceberg lettuce

assorted herb sprigs

for the filling

25g (1oz) bean-thread (transparent) noodles

1 small onion

10g (¼ oz) Chinese dried mushrooms

1 tbsp groundnut oil

2 tbsp chopped garlic

2 tbsp finely chopped spring onions

2 tbsp chopped shallots

225g (8oz) minced pork

1½ tsp salt

½ tsp freshly ground black pepper

100g (4oz) cooked fresh crab meat

for the dipping sauce

1–2 fresh red chillies

2 tbsp fish sauce (nam pla)

1 tbsp chopped garlic

1 tbsp lemon juice

1 tbsp sugar

31

Fresh Vietnamese Spring Rolls

I love these unusual, sparkling-fresh spring rolls. They make a perfect starter and I have often served them as a main course, especially on hot, humid summer evenings.

Serves 4–8

350g (12oz) raw prawns, shelled and de-veined

50g (2oz) bean-thread (transparent) noodles

225g (8oz) soft salad leaves

large bunches fresh basil, mint and coriander

1 packet 20cm (8in) round rice paper wrappers

225g (8oz) fresh beansprouts, rinsed

for the peanut dipping sauce

2 tbsp fish sauce (nam pla)

1–2 fresh red chillies, de-seeded and chopped

1 tbsp finely chopped garlic

2 tbsp lime or lemon juice

5 tbsp water

1 tbsp sugar

3 tbsp roasted peanuts, crushed

Step one First make the peanut dipping sauce. Combine all the ingredients except the peanuts in a blender and process thoroughly. Pour into a small bowl and leave to stand for at least 10 minutes before using (the sauce can be prepared several hours in advance, if necessary).

Step two Blanch the prawns in a pan of boiling salted water for 3 minutes, drain well and then cut them in half lengthways. Set aside until needed.

Step three Soak the noodles in a large bowl of hot water for 15 minutes, until soft, then drain. Cut them into 7.5cm (3in) lengths, using scissors or a knife. Wash the salad leaves well and spin them dry in a salad spinner. Do the same with the basil, mint and coriander.

Step four When you are ready to make the spring rolls, fill a large bowl with warm water. Dip one of the rice paper rounds in the water and let it soften, then remove and drain on a tea-towel. Put a large salad leaf on the softened rice paper wrapper. Add a spoonful of the noodles to the salad leaf, then add 3 basil leaves and 3 mint leaves. Then carefully roll the rice paper halfway up. Now place 3 pieces of prawn, 3 coriander sprigs and 2 tablespoons beansprouts on the wrapper. Fold the 2 ends in, then keep rolling until the entire rice paper is rolled up. Repeat with all the remaining ingredients. Cover the spring rolls with a damp tea-towel until you are ready to serve them (do not refrigerate; they are meant to be served at room temperature).

Step five Just before serving, stir the crushed peanuts into the sauce. Cut each spring roll in half on the diagonal and serve with the sauce.

Malaysian Fish Curry

I have eaten this wonderfully fragrant curry many times in Malaysia, where fresh fish is a standard item in every home and on every restaurant menu. It makes an ideal quick meal. This savoury, delectable treat goes perfectly with plain rice (see page 64).

Step one Cut the fish into 5cm (2in) pieces and set aside.

Step two For the curry paste, put the onions, ginger, garlic, curry paste, coriander, fennel seeds, turmeric and lemon juice in a food-processor. Add half the coconut milk and blend well.

Step three Pour the remaining coconut milk into a wok or saucepan and add the curry paste. Bring the mixture to a simmer and cook for 5 minutes. Add the fish pieces and cook for another 5 minutes. Serve at once.

Serves 2–4

450g (1lb) firm white fish fillets, such as cod, halibut or sea bass, skinned

for the curry paste

175g (6oz) onions, coarsely chopped

1½ tbsp finely chopped fresh root ginger

1 tbsp finely chopped garlic

2 tbsp Madras curry paste

1 tsp ground coriander

½ tsp ground fennel seeds

½ tsp ground turmeric

2 tbsp lemon juice

150ml (5fl oz) tinned coconut milk

Fragrant Singapore-style Prawn Curry

I enjoyed this delightful stir-fry dish for the first time in Singapore some years ago. Prawns have a delicate yet distinctive flavour, and the clean, mildly citrus touch of the lemon grass makes a perfect counterpart. The quick cooking style ensures that the two main ingredients remain at their best. Use fresh lemon grass whenever possible – in a dish like this it is worth a detour to obtain it. But if your search is in vain, you could substitute 2 tablespoons of grated lemon zest.

Serves 2–4

1 fresh stick
of lemon grass

1 fresh red
or green chilli

2 tbsp groundnut oil

100g (4oz) onion,
coarsely chopped

2 tbsp finely
chopped garlic

2 tsp finely chopped
fresh root ginger

450g (1lb) raw
prawns, shelled and
de-veined, tails on

2 tsp Madras
curry paste

1 tsp chilli bean sauce

1 tsp sugar

2 tbsp water

1 tbsp Shaoxing rice
wine or dry sherry

2 tsp light soy sauce

½ tsp salt

¼ tsp freshly ground
black pepper

fresh coriander
sprigs or lime
wedges, to garnish

Step one Peel off the tough outer layers of the lemon grass stick, leaving the tender, whitish centre. Chop it finely. Cut the chilli in half and carefully remove and discard the seeds. Chop the chilli finely and combine it with the lemon grass.

Step two Heat a wok or large frying pan over a high heat. Add the oil and, when it is very hot and slightly smoking, add the onion, garlic, ginger, lemon grass and chilli and stir-fry for 1 minute. Then add the prawns and stir-fry for another minute.

Step three Now add all the remaining ingredients, except the coriander or lime wedges, and stir-fry for 4 minutes or until the prawns are firm and cooked. Turn the mixture onto a warm serving platter, garnish and serve at once.

Red Curry Prawns

This is a tasty version of a classic Thai dish, *gaeng phed ghoong*. Once the sauce is made, the prawns cook in just minutes. Serve with plain steamed rice (see page 64).

Step one Heat a wok or large frying pan until it is very hot and add the oil. When it is hot, add the garlic, shallots and cumin seeds and stir-fry for 5 minutes or until well toasted. Then add the shrimp paste and curry paste and stir-fry for another 2 minutes.

Step two Now add the coconut milk, fish sauce or soy sauce, sugar, basil leaves and lime leaves or zest. Reduce the heat and simmer for 5 minutes.

Step three Add the prawns and cook for 5 minutes, stirring from time to time. Add the coriander leaves and give the mixture a good stir, then serve.

Serves 4

1½ tbsp vegetable oil

3 tbsp coarsely chopped garlic

2 tbsp finely sliced shallots

2 tsp cumin seeds

1 tsp shrimp paste

1½ tbsp Thai red curry paste

1 x 400ml (14fl oz) tin coconut milk

1 tbsp fish sauce (nam pla) or light soy sauce

2 tsp sugar

a small handful of fresh Thai basil leaves or ordinary basil leaves, shredded

4 kaffir lime leaves or 1 tbsp shredded lime zest

450g (1lb) raw prawns, shelled and de-veined, tails on

a handful of fresh coriander leaves, chopped

Green Curry Prawns

This delectable dish is quick and easy to make. The fiery green curry is mellowed by the rich sweetness of coconut milk. It makes a wonderful meal when served with plain steamed rice (see page 64). In Thailand, it is known as *gaeng kheow wan ghoong*.

Serves 4

1 fresh stick of lemon grass

1½ tbsp vegetable oil

2 tbsp Thai green curry paste

4 kaffir lime leaves, torn, or 1 tbsp shredded lime zest

2 tbsp fish sauce (nam pla) or light soy sauce

2 tsp sugar

1 x 400ml (14fl oz) tin coconut milk

450g (1lb) raw prawns, shelled and de-veined, tails on

a small handful of fresh Thai basil leaves or ordinary basil leaves, shredded

Step one Peel off the tough outer layers of the lemon grass stick, leaving the tender whitish centre. Slice it finely.

Step two Heat a wok or large frying pan until it is very hot and add the oil. Now add the green curry paste and stir-fry for 2 minutes.

Step three Add the lemon grass, lime leaves or zest, fish sauce or soy sauce, sugar and coconut milk. Reduce the heat and simmer for 5 minutes.

Step four Add the prawns and cook for 5 minutes, stirring from time to time. Add the basil leaves and give the mixture a good stir. Serve at once.

Red Pork Curry

Gaeng phed moo is a quick and easy Thai curry. The assertive spices and seasonings enhance this classic treatment for pork.

Step one Cut the pork into thin slices about 5cm (2in) long and set aside.

Step two Heat a wok or large frying pan over a medium heat and add the oil. When it is hot, add the curry paste and stir-fry for 30 seconds. Add the pork slices, turn up the heat and stir-fry them for 1 minute or until they are entirely coated with the curry paste. Remove with a slotted spoon and set aside.

Step three Add the galangal or ginger, turmeric and garlic to the wok and stir-fry for 10 seconds. Stir in the coconut milk, fish sauce, lime leaves or zest and sugar, bring to the boil and simmer for 5 minutes.

Step four Return the pork to the sauce and simmer for 3 minutes or until it is cooked through. Toss in the basil and give it a final stir. Serve at once.

Serves 4

450g (1lb) pork fillet

1½ tbsp vegetable oil

2 tbsp Thai red curry paste

3 tbsp finely shredded fresh galangal or root ginger

1 tsp ground turmeric

2 tbsp finely sliced garlic

1 x 400ml (14fl oz) tin coconut milk

2 tbsp fish sauce (nam pla)

4 kaffir lime leaves or 1 tbsp shredded lime zest

2 tsp sugar

a handful of fresh Thai basil leaves or ordinary basil leaves

For more recipes from My Kitchen Table, sign up for our newsletter at www.mykitchentable.co.uk/newsletter

Vietnamese-style Beef Stew

This hearty dish is perfect for a cold winter's night. It takes a little time to cook, but can happily bubble away while you get on with other things.

Serves 4–6

6 sticks of lemon grass

1.5kg (3lb) stewing beef, such as brisket

1 small onion

4 spring onions

450g (1lb) carrots

2 tbsp groundnut oil

6 slices fresh root ginger

6 garlic cloves, lightly crushed

2–3 tsp crushed dried red chilli

coarsely chopped fresh basil and mint, to garnish

for the braising sauce

900ml (1½ pints) home-made chicken stock (see page 7) or good-quality bought stock

75g (3oz) sugar

3 tbsp light soy sauce

2 tbsp dark soy sauce

3 tbsp Shaoxing rice wine or dry sherry

4 star anise

2 tsp five-spice powder

2 tbsp tomato purée

2 tsp salt

1 tsp freshly ground black pepper

Step one Peel off the tough outer layers of the lemon grass sticks, leaving the tender, whitish centre. Crush with the flat of a knife, then cut into 7.5cm (3in) pieces. Cut the beef into 5cm (2in) cubes. Coarsely chop the onion and cut the spring onions on a slight diagonal into 5cm (2in) lengths. Peel the carrots and cut them on a slight diagonal into 5cm (2in) lengths.

Step two Heat a wok or large frying pan, add the oil and, when it is very hot and slightly smoking, add half the beef. Fry for about 10 minutes, until browned all over, then remove with a slotted spoon and set aside. Repeat with the remaining beef.

Step three Pour off most of the excess oil from the wok, leaving about 2 tablespoons. Add the lemon grass, onion, spring onions, ginger, garlic and dried chilli and stir-fry for 5 minutes. Transfer this mixture to a large casserole or saucepan. Add the browned beef and all the ingredients for the braising sauce. Bring to the boil, skim off any fat from the surface, then reduce the heat to a low simmer. Cover and braise for 1½–2 hours.

Step four Add the carrots and continue to cook for 30 minutes, until the beef and carrots are tender. Remove the beef and carrots with a slotted spoon and set aside. Turn the heat up to high and boil the liquid rapidly for about 15 minutes, until reduced and slightly thickened. Garnish with the chopped basil and mint and serve immediately. The stew can also be left to cool and then reheated later, garnished and served.

Indonesian Dried Beef Curry

Known as *rendang*, this is probably one of Indonesia's most famous dishes. It appears on restaurant menus, as well as in many homes, and is unlike any other curry I have experienced. The meat is cooked in a highly aromatic sauce until the curry is dry. It is perfect for entertaining a large crowd, as you can put it on to cook before your guests arrive and simply serve up when it is ready. Serve with plain rice (see page 64) and a vegetable or salad.

Step one Put half the onion slices in a blender with the ginger, garlic and 3–4 tablespoons of the coconut milk and blend until smooth. Put the meat in a large bowl, pour over the mixture from the blender and mix until the meat is thoroughly coated.

Step two Heat a wok or large frying pan, add the oil and, when it is very hot and slightly smoking, add the remaining onion. Stir-fry until golden brown. Using a slotted spoon, transfer the onion to a large casserole or saucepan.

Step three Add half the meat to the wok and fry for about 10 minutes, until browned all over. Using a slotted spoon, transfer to the pan with the onions. Repeat with the remaining beef.

Step four Add all the remaining ingredients, except the lemon juice, to the pan. Bring to a simmer and reduce the heat as low as possible. Slowly braise, uncovered, for 2½–3 hours, stirring occasionally, until the beef is tender.

Step five Stir in the lemon juice. The sauce should be quite thick now – almost dry. You can serve the curry immediately or you can leave it to cool and reheat it later.

Serves 4–6

2 onions, sliced

1 tbsp coarsely chopped fresh root ginger

6 garlic cloves, lightly crushed

1.2 litres (2 pints) tinned coconut milk

1kg (2¼ lb) stewing beef (or lamb), such as brisket or shin, cut into 5cm (2in) cubes

2 tbsp groundnut oil

2–3 tsp crushed dried red chilli

5 cloves

1 cinnamon stick

2 tsp salt

1 tsp freshly ground black pepper

1 tbsp ground coriander

1 tsp ground cumin

1 tsp ground ginger

4 tbsp lemon juice

Malaysian Vegetable Curry

Although one can detect an Indian influence in this typical Malaysian dish, the flavours are unique. What makes a great difference is the use of shrimp paste, an aromatic seasoning found in many Malaysian vegetable dishes. When it is combined with chillies, the results are sensational. There is a secret, however, to this recipe: do not add all the vegetables at the same time. Like stir-frying, stewing requires you to give different vegetables different cooking times. If the cooking times are properly observed, the whole dish comes out perfectly done.

Serves 4

2 x 400ml (14fl oz) tins coconut milk

100g (4oz) onion, finely sliced

1 tbsp finely chopped garlic

½ tsp shrimp paste

½ tsp ground turmeric

2 fresh red or green chillies, de-seeded and sliced

1 tsp salt

½ tsp freshly ground black pepper

175g (6oz) potatoes, peeled and thickly sliced

350g (12oz) Chinese leaves (Peking cabbage), shredded

1 tbsp lemon juice

Step one Pour the coconut milk into a wok or large frying pan and bring to a simmer. Add the onion, garlic, shrimp paste, turmeric, chillies, salt and pepper and return to a simmer.

Step two Add the potatoes and cook for 8 minutes, until they are almost tender, then add the Chinese leaves. Cover and simmer for 6 minutes, until they are thoroughly cooked. Stir in the lemon juice and serve immediately.

Malaysian Curry Mee

Malaysia is a culinary crossroads of cuisines, spices and ingredients, with Chinese and Indian flavours in particular merging into a distinctly national style of cooking. A popular Malaysian recipe is this simple but delectable egg noodle dish (the word *mee* refers to the noodles). It combines beansprouts and beancurd – standard ingredients used by Chinese cooks – with a light curry sauce that manifests the Indian influence. It makes a delicious one-dish meal all by itself.

Step one Cut the beancurd into 2.5cm (1in) cubes, then leave on kitchen paper to drain for 30 minutes.

Step two Cook the noodles for 3–5 minutes in a pan of boiling water, until tender. Drain and plunge them into cold water. Drain again thoroughly and toss them with the vegetable oil, then set aside.

Step three Heat a wok or large frying pan over a high heat. Add the groundnut oil and, when it is very hot and slightly smoking, add the dried chillies and stir-fry for 20 seconds. Push the chillies to the side of the wok, reduce the heat and add the beancurd cubes. Brown slowly on each side.

Step four Add the garlic and onion and stir-fry for 3 minutes, until the onion is soft. Now add the coconut milk, turmeric, curry powder, salt, sugar, light and dark soy sauce and some black pepper and simmer for 4 minutes.

Step five Finally, add the noodles and beansprouts, cook for 2 minutes and mix well. Serve at once.

Serves 4

450g (1lb) firm beancurd

225g (8oz) dried or fresh Chinese egg noodles

1 tbsp vegetable oil

2 tbsp groundnut oil

2 dried red chillies, halved

2 tbsp coarsely chopped garlic

100g (4oz) onion, finely chopped

400ml (14fl oz) tinned coconut milk

¼ tsp ground turmeric

2 tbsp Madras curry powder

1 tsp salt

1 tsp sugar

2 tbsp light soy sauce

1 tbsp dark soy sauce

freshly ground black pepper

225g (8oz) fresh beansprouts, rinsed

Sweet and Sour Pork, Chiu Chow Style

Use tinned lychees for this delicious sweet and sour pork dish.

Serves 4

450g (1lb) minced
fatty pork

1 egg white

175g (6oz) water
chestnuts

2 tbsp light soy sauce

1 tbsp dark soy sauce

2 tbsp Shaoxing rice
wine or dry sherry

1½ tbsp sugar

2 tsp salt

½ tsp freshly ground
black pepper

100g (4oz) carrots

100g (4oz) each green
and red pepper

cornflour, for dusting

600ml (1 pint)
groundnut oil

4 spring onions

75g (3oz) lychees

for the sauce

150ml (5fl oz) chicken
stock (see page 7)

1 tbsp light soy sauce

2 tsp dark soy sauce

2 tsp sesame oil

¼ tsp each salt and
white pepper

1½ tbsp Chinese
white rice vinegar or
cider vinegar

1 tbsp sugar

2 tbsp tomato ketchup

2 tsp cornflour

Step one Mix the pork with the egg white and 4 tablespoons water, using your hand (this helps incorporate air). The mixture should be light and fluffy. Do not use a blender as it would make it too dense. Coarsely chop the water chestnuts and add them to the mixture along with the light and dark soy sauce, rice wine or sherry, sugar, salt and pepper and mix thoroughly.

Step two With your hands, shape the mixture into small rounds, about the size of golf balls.

Step three Thinly slice the carrots on the diagonal and cut the peppers into 2.5cm (1in) squares. Bring a pan of water to the boil and blanch the carrots and peppers for about 4 minutes, until just tender. Drain and set aside.

Step four Dust the pork balls with cornflour, shaking off any excess. Heat the oil in a deep-fat fryer or large wok until slightly smoking. Reduce the heat to moderate and deep-fry the pork balls for 3–4 minutes, until crisp and cooked through. Remove with a slotted spoon and drain on kitchen paper.

Step five In a large saucepan, combine all the sauce ingredients, except the cornflour, and bring to the boil. Slice the spring onions into 2.5cm (1in) pieces and add them along with the carrots and peppers, and stir well. Mix the cornflour with 1 tablespoon water, add this mixture to the pan and cook for 2 minutes, then reduce the heat so that the mixture is simmering. Drain the lychees and add them along with the pork balls to the sauce. Mix well, then serve at once, garnished with coriander leaves.

Indonesian Beancurd with Peanuts

Although beancurd probably originated in China, it was brought to Indonesia by Chinese immigrants and embraced by local cooks. Here it is paired with peanuts, a very Indonesian food.

Step one Cut the beancurd into 2.5cm (1in) cubes, then leave on kitchen paper to drain for 30 minutes.

Step two Heat the 450ml (15fl oz) oil in a large wok until it is almost smoking, then deep-fry the beancurd cubes in 2 batches. When each batch is lightly browned, remove and drain well on kitchen paper. Let the cooking oil cool and then discard it.

Step three Wipe the wok clean and reheat it over a high heat. Add the 1½ tablespoons of oil and, when it is very hot and smoking, add the peanut butter, garlic, chillies and shrimp paste and stir-fry for 1 minute.

Step four Add the drained beancurd. Stir-fry for 30 seconds, then add the dark soy sauce, lemon juice, sugar and coconut milk. Reduce the heat to low and simmer the mixture slowly for 8 minutes.

Step five Raise the heat again and cook until most of the liquid has evaporated. Place the beancurd on a serving platter, cover with the beansprouts, then sprinkle on the peanuts and spring onion. Serve at once.

Serves 4

450g (1lb) firm beancurd

450ml (15fl oz) groundnut oil for deep-frying, plus 1½ tbsp

3 tbsp peanut butter

2 tbsp coarsely chopped garlic

2 small fresh red chillies, de-seeded and chopped

1 tsp shrimp paste

2 tbsp dark soy sauce

3 tbsp lemon juice

1 tsp sugar

250ml (8fl oz) tinned coconut milk

to garnish

100g (4oz) fresh beansprouts, rinsed

50g (2oz) roasted peanuts, coarsely chopped

1 spring onion, shredded

Chicken Thigh Casserole with Orange

The Chinese buy their chickens live to ensure that they are at their freshest when cooked. Obviously, this is not practical in the West. Commercially produced chickens tend to lack taste and frozen chicken is especially bland and should be avoided whenever possible. Try to buy fresh chicken for Chinese cooking. It should have a healthy, pinkish colour, a fresh smell and be firm in texture. If possible, buy free-range or corn-fed – not only have they been raised by more humane methods, but their flavour is far superior.

Serves 4

1½ tbsp groundnut oil

900g (2lb) skinless chicken thighs

1 tbsp finely chopped garlic

1 tbsp finely chopped fresh root ginger

2 tbsp black beans, drained

2 tsp orange zest, cut into thin strips

150ml (¼ pint) fresh orange juice

2 tbsp light soy sauce

2 tsp chilli bean sauce

Step one Heat a large, heavy, flameproof casserole, then add the oil and quickly brown the chicken thighs on both sides. Push to the side of the casserole, then add the garlic, ginger, black beans and orange zest and stir for 30 seconds.

Step two Add the orange juice, soy sauce and chilli bean sauce, bring to the boil, then reduce the heat to a simmer. Cover the casserole tightly and cook for 20 minutes or until the chicken is done. Check by piercing with a skewer; the juices should run clear. Serve at once.

Mussels in Coconut Curry Sauce

Mussels are an ideal quick and easy food and they tend to be quite economical. Once they have been scrubbed clean in cold water to remove all sand, they cook very rapidly, announcing that they are ready by opening their shells. Make sure they are firmly sealed before cooking; throw away any that do not close up when tapped against a work surface. Mussels are very much a seafood, redolent of salty tides. They are therefore prime candidates for a robust and distinctive sauce. It is an ideal dish to serve with plain steamed rice. This simple dish can easily be increased for larger gatherings. I prefer to use smaller mussels, so if you have a choice, try them.

Step one Scrub the mussels under cold running water and scrape off any barnacles with a small knife. Pull out and discard the fibrous 'beards'. Discard any open mussels that don't close when tapped lightly on a work surface.

Step two Heat a wok or large frying pan over a high heat. Add the oil and, when it is very hot and slightly smoking, add the garlic, ginger and spring onions and stir-fry for 20 seconds, then add the mussels and stir-fry for 1 minute.

Step three Add the curry powder or paste, fish sauce, sugar, coconut milk and water, cover and continue to cook for 5 minutes or until all the mussels have opened. Discard any that do not open. Give the mixture a final stir and serve at once.

Serves 4–6

1.5kg (3lb) fresh mussels

1½ tbsp groundnut oil

3 tbsp coarsely chopped garlic

2 tbsp finely chopped fresh root ginger

2 tbsp finely chopped spring onions

2 tbsp Madras curry powder or paste

2 tbsp fish sauce (nam pla)

1 tsp sugar

400ml (15fl oz) tinned coconut milk

3 tbsp water

59

Vietnamese-style Chicken Curry

In this fragrant dish, the chicken is marinated in a curry paste, then stir-fried with vegetables. It is delicious and goes perfectly with plain rice.

Serves 4

450g (1lb) boneless, skinless chicken thighs

2 tbsp groundnut oil

2 onions, cut into eighths

300ml (10fl oz) home-made chicken stock (see page 7) or good-quality bought stock

400ml (14fl oz) tinned coconut milk

4 fresh tomatoes, cut into quarters

a handful of fresh coriander sprigs, to garnish (optional)

for the marinade

2 fresh sticks of lemon grass

4 whole garlic cloves

2 red or green chillies, de-seeded and chopped

2 tsp sugar

1 tbsp Madras curry paste

2 tbsp Madras curry powder

1 tsp salt

½ tsp freshly ground black pepper

3 tbsp fish sauce (nam pla)

1 tbsp water

Step one Cut the chicken into about 5cm (2in) chunks.

Step two To make the marinade, peel the lemon grass stick to reveal the tender, whitish centre. Crush it with the flat of a knife, then cut it into small chunks. In a food-processor, combine the garlic, chillies, sugar, curry paste, curry powder, salt, pepper, fish sauce and water and blend to a paste. Mix this with the lemon grass and chicken pieces, and stir until all the pieces are thoroughly coated. Leave the chicken to marinate for about 1 hour at room temperature.

Step three Heat a wok or large frying pan over a high heat. Add the oil and, when it is very hot and slightly smoking, reduce the heat to medium, add the chicken and stir-fry for 5 minutes or until it begins to brown. Add the onions and stir-fry for 3 minutes. Add the stock and coconut milk. Bring the mixture to a simmer, reduce the heat and simmer uncovered for 10 minutes. Then add the tomatoes, stir well and continue to cook for another 2 minutes. Transfer the contents to a bowl, garnish with coriander, if using, and serve.

Rainbow Vegetables with Curry

Mild curry dishes with vegetables are popular in Hong Kong. The particular spices in curry add an exotic taste that is quite a change from the usual garlic and/or ginger most commonly used in Chinese cookery. This assortment of differently coloured vegetables (hence the name) is usually served at banquets. But there is no need to wait for a special occasion to enjoy such a vegetarian taste treat.

Step one Cut the Chinese leaves into 4cm (1½in) strips. Then cut the Chinese greens into 4cm (1½in) pieces. Peel and cut the carrots on the diagonal into 4cm (1½in) x 5mm (¼in) segments. Cut the asparagus on the diagonal into 4cm (1½in) pieces.

Step two In a large pan of boiling salted water, blanch the leaves for about 5 minutes. Remove them with a slotted spoon and drain thoroughly. Then blanch the Chinese greens for 3 minutes in the same water. Remove and drain. Now blanch the carrots for 5 minutes and the asparagus for 3 minutes. Remove and drain thoroughly. Arrange the blanched vegetables on a warm serving platter.

Step three Heat a wok or large frying pan over a high heat. Add the oil and, when it is very hot and slightly smoking, add the shallots and stir-fry for 1 minute. Then add the curry paste and coconut milk. Bring the mixture to the boil and add the sugar, salt and Shaoxing rice wine or dry sherry. Stir to mix well. Finally, add the sesame oil. Pour the sauce over the platter of vegetables and serve at once.

Serves 4

225g (8oz) Chinese leaves (Peking cabbage)

225g (8oz) Chinese greens, such as Chinese flowering cabbage or pak choy

225g (8oz) carrots

225g (8oz) asparagus

for the sauce

1 tbsp groundnut oil

2 tbsp finely chopped shallots

1½ tbsp Madras curry paste

300ml (10fl oz) tinned coconut milk

2 tsp sugar

2 tsp salt

1 tbsp Shaoxing rice wine or dry sherry

2 tsp sesame oil

For a video masterclass on chopping vegetables, go to
www.mykitchentable.co.uk/videos/choppingvegetables

63

Perfect Steamed Rice

The Chinese way of steaming rice is simple, direct and effective. I prefer to use long-grain white rice, which is dry and fluffy when cooked. Don't use precooked or 'easy-cook' rice, as it lacks the texture and starchy taste fundamental to Chinese rice. The secret of preparing rice without it becoming sticky is to cook it first in an uncovered pan at a high heat until most of the water has evaporated. Then the heat should be turned very low, the pan covered and the rice cooked slowly in the remaining steam. Never uncover the pan once the steaming process has begun; just time it and wait. Here is a good trick to remember: if you cover the rice with about 2.5cm (1in) of water, it should always cook properly without sticking. Many packet recipes for rice use too much water and result in a gluey mess. Follow my method and you will have perfect steamed rice, the easy Chinese way.

Serves 4

enough long-grain rice to fill a glass measuring jug to 400ml (14fl oz)

600ml (1 pint) water

Step one Put the rice into a large bowl and wash it in several changes of water until the water becomes clear.

Step two Drain the rice. Put in a heavy pan with the 600ml (1 pint) water and bring to the boil. Boil for about 5 minutes until most of the surface liquid has evaporated. The surface of the rice should have small indentations, like a pitted crater. At this point, cover the pan with a very tight-fitting lid, reduce the heat to as low as possible and leave the rice to cook undisturbed for 15 minutes. There is no need to 'fluff' the rice; just let it rest off the heat for 5 minutes before serving.

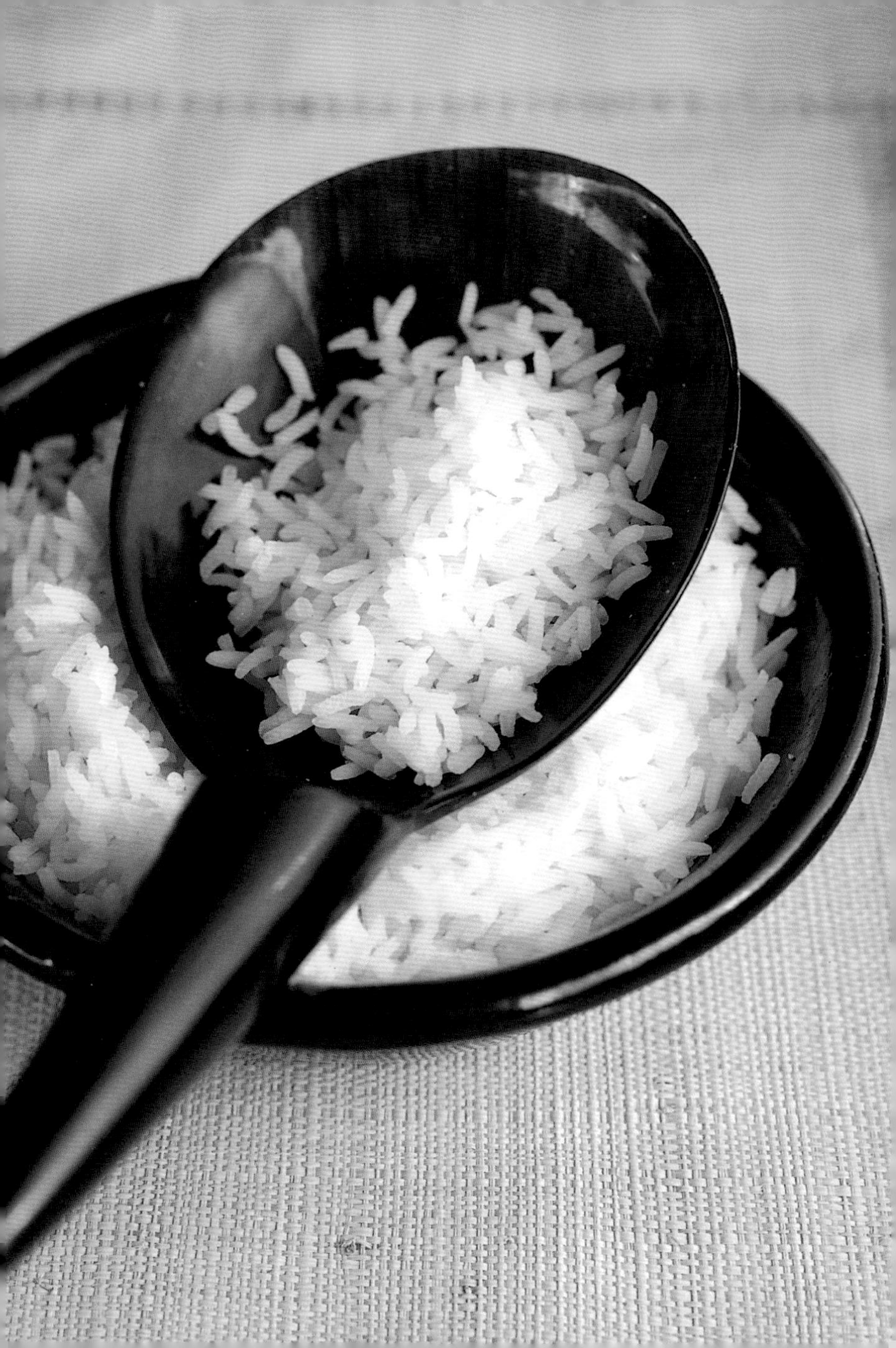

Steamed Cantonese-style Fish

Steaming is a favourite Chinese cooking method for fish. A simple but gentle technique, it doesn't mask the fresh taste of the fish, which remains moist and tender. An added bonus is that it is a very healthy way to cook. Always buy the freshest possible fish and ask your fishmonger to prepare it for cooking.

Step one Pat the fish dry with kitchen paper and evenly rub with the salt, rubbing it inside the cavity as well, if you are using a whole fish. Put the fish on a heatproof plate and scatter the ginger evenly over the top.

Step two Set up a steamer or put a rack into a wok or deep pan. Fill it with 5cm (2in) of water and bring to the boil over a high heat. Put the plate of fish on the rack, cover tightly and steam the fish until it is just cooked. Flat fish fillets will take about 5 minutes; whole fish, or thick fillets such as sea bass, will take 12–14 minutes. The fish should turn opaque and flake slightly, but still remain moist.

Step three Remove the plate of cooked fish and pour off any liquid that may have accumulated. Scatter the spring onions on the fish, then drizzle over the light and dark soy sauces.

Step four Heat the two oils together in a small saucepan until smoking, then immediately pour them over the fish. Garnish with coriander sprigs and serve at once.

Serves 4

450g (1lb) firm white fish fillets, such as cod or sole, skinned, or a whole fish, such as sole or turbot

1 tsp coarse sea salt or ordinary cooking salt

1½ tbsp finely shredded fresh root ginger

3 tbsp finely shredded spring onions

2 tbsp light soy sauce

2 tsp dark soy sauce

1 tbsp groundnut oil

2 tsp sesame oil

fresh coriander sprigs, to garnish

Sichuan Braised Fish

This quick and easy dish is bursting with the spicy flavours of Sichuan. A firm, white fish, such as cod, sea bass, halibut or haddock, is most suitable for braising.

Serves 4

450g (1lb) fresh firm white fish fillets, such as cod, sea bass, halibut or haddock, skinned

1 tsp salt

cornflour for dusting

150ml (5fl oz) groundnut oil

3 spring onions, cut on the diagonal into 5cm (2in) slices

1 tbsp finely chopped garlic

2 tsp finely chopped fresh root ginger

for the sauce

150ml (5fl oz) home-made chicken stock (see page 7) or good-quality bought stock

1 tsp whole yellow bean sauce

1 tbsp chilli bean sauce

2 tbsp Shaoxing rice wine or dry sherry

2 tsp dark soy sauce

2 tsp sugar

2 tsp sesame oil

½ tsp salt

¼ tsp freshly ground white pepper

Step one Sprinkle the fish fillets evenly on both sides with the salt. Cut them into strips 5 x 2.5cm (2 x 1in) and leave for 20 minutes.

Step two Dust the strips of fish liberally with cornflour.

Step three Heat a wok over a high heat. Add the oil and, when it is very hot and slightly smoking, reduce the heat. Fry the pieces of fish on both sides until they are lightly browned. Remove from the wok and drain on kitchen paper.

Step four Pour off most of the oil, leaving about a tablespoon in the wok. Reheat the wok, then add the spring onions, garlic and ginger and stir-fry for 30 seconds.

Step five Add all the sauce ingredients and bring to the boil. Reduce the heat to a simmer and return the fish to the pan. Simmer for about 2–3 minutes, gently turning the fish in the sauce, then serve.

Steamed Fresh Oysters

Steaming oysters brings out their subtle, briny taste and wonderful texture. Watch them carefully to prevent overcooking. This dish is very simple to prepare and is perfect for a weeknight meal.

Step one Scrub the oysters clean. You will have to steam them in 2 batches, so divide them between 2 heatproof plates.

Step two Next set up a steamer or put a rack into a wok or deep pan and fill it with 5cm (2in) of water. Bring the water to the boil over a high heat. Put one plate of oysters into the steamer or on the rack, turn the heat to low and cover the wok or pan tightly. Steam the oysters gently for 5 minutes or until they are open.

Step three Meanwhile, combine all the sauce ingredients, except the groundnut oil, in a heatproof bowl. Heat a small pan over a high heat. Add the oil and, when it is very hot and slightly smoking, pour it over the sauce ingredients.

Step four Remove the oysters from the steamer and cook the second batch. Give the sauce several good stirs. Remove the top shell of the oysters and pour a little sauce over each. Garnish with coriander sprigs and serve.

Serves 4

16 large fresh oysters in the shell

fresh coriander sprigs, to garnish

for the sauce

2 tsp finely chopped garlic

1 tbsp finely chopped fresh root ginger

1 tsp chilli bean sauce

1 tbsp Shaoxing rice wine or dry sherry

1 tbsp light soy sauce

2 tsp dark soy sauce

2 fresh red chillies, de-seeded and chopped

3 tbsp finely shredded spring onions

3 tbsp groundnut oil

Singapore-style Steamed Fish

One of the highlights of eating in Singapore is tasting Nonya cuisine. This fantastic and intriguing cooking style comes from the Babas, a mixture of ethnic Chinese and Malays – one of the first fusion cuisines, if you like. Many of the dishes combine Chinese subtlety with the assertive flavours of Malaysian cooking. Here is one example of their many contributions. Only the freshest fish will do.

Serves 4

450g (1lb) firm white fish fillets, such as cod or sole, or 1 whole fish, such as sole or turbot, weighing 675–900g (1½–2lb)

1 tsp coarse sea salt or ordinary cooking salt

15g (½oz) Chinese dried mushrooms

3 tbsp Chinese preserved vegetables

2 tbsp light soy sauce

freshly ground black pepper

to garnish

a handful of fresh coriander sprigs

3 tbsp finely shredded spring onions

Step one Pat the fish fillets or whole fish dry with kitchen paper. Rub evenly with the salt and some pepper (inside and outside if you are using a whole fish), then set aside.

Step two Soak the mushrooms in warm water for 20 minutes, then drain and squeeze out excess liquid. Remove and discard the stalks and finely shred the caps into thin strips. Soak the Chinese preserved vegetables in water for 10 minutes to remove some of the salt, then drain and finely shred them.

Step three Next set up a steamer, or put a rack into a wok or deep pan and fill it with 5cm (2in) of water. Bring the water to the boil over a high heat. Put the fish on a heatproof plate and scatter the mushrooms and preserved vegetables evenly over the top. Sprinkle the soy sauce over all.

Step four Put the plate of fish into the steamer or on to the rack. Cover the pan tightly and gently steam the fish until it is just cooked. Flat fish fillets will take about 5 minutes to cook; whole fish or fillets such as sea bass will take 12–14 minutes. When it is done, the fish will turn opaque and flake slightly, but should still remain moist. Remove the plate of cooked fish and scatter the coriander and spring onions on top. Serve at once.

Braised Clams with Chilli and Basil

This is one of the easiest Thai recipes. Clams cook quickly and have an assertive seafood flavour, made even more distinctive here by the addition of fresh basil and chillies. If clams are unavailable, you could substitute mussels and the dish will be just as delectable. Its Thai name is *hoy lai phad prik.*

Step one Scrub the clams under cold running water, discarding any open ones that do not close when tapped lightly on a work surface.

Step two Heat a wok or large frying pan over a high heat and add the oil. When it is very hot and slightly smoking, add the garlic, shallots, chillies and clams and stir-fry them for 3–4 minutes, until the clams begin to open.

Step three Add the fish sauce or soy sauce, then reduce the heat, cover the pan and cook for 3 minutes. Stir in the basil leaves and serve at once.

Serves 4

1kg (2¼ lb) fresh clams

1½ tbsp vegetable oil

3 tbsp coarsely chopped garlic

2 tbsp finely chopped shallots

3 large, fresh red or green chillies, de-seeded and shredded

2 tbsp fish sauce (nam pla) or light soy sauce

a handful of fresh Thai basil leaves or ordinary basil leaves

Have you made this recipe? Tell us what you think at
www.mykitchentable.co.uk/blog

Seafood in Coconut Milk

Thailand enjoys a bountiful supply of seafood from her long coastline, leading to an abundance of relatively inexpensive fish and shellfish dishes such as this one, known as *hor mok talay*. Bracing seasonings and rich coconut milk bring out the best in seafood. Like the Thais, use whatever is freshest on the day you are cooking.

Serves 4–6

1.5–1.6kg (3–3½ lb) freshly cooked crab in the shell

175g (6oz) fresh mussels

3 fresh sticks of lemon grass

4 garlic cloves, crushed

4 tbsp finely sliced shallots

3 tbsp chopped fresh coriander

2 small, fresh red or green Thai chillies, de-seeded and chopped

1 tbsp black peppercorns

2 tsp shredded lime zest

2 x 400ml (14fl oz) tins coconut milk

175g (6oz) raw unshelled prawns

175g (6oz) fresh scallops including the corals

2 tbsp fish sauce (nam pla)

2 tbsp lime juice

2 tbsp sugar

Step one Remove the tail flap, stomach sac and feathery gills from the cooked crab, if necessary. Using a heavy knife or cleaver, cut the crab, shell included, into large pieces.

Step two Scrub the mussels under cold running water and scrape off any barnacles with a small knife. Pull out and discard the fibrous 'beards'. Discard any open mussels that don't close when tapped lightly on a work surface.

Step three Peel off the tough outer layers of the lemon grass sticks, leaving the tender whitish centre. Chop it finely and place in a blender with the garlic, shallots, coriander, chillies, black peppercorns and lime zest. Add about 3 tablespoons of the coconut milk and blend to a paste.

Step four Pour the remaining coconut milk into a wok or deep pan and bring to the boil. Reduce the heat, stir in the blended spice paste and simmer for 3 minutes.

Step five Add the crab, mussels, prawns, scallops, fish sauce, lime juice and sugar, then cover and simmer for 10 minutes. Turn the mixture on to a large platter and serve. It is perfectly good manners to eat the crab, prawns and mussels with your fingers, but I suggest that you have a bowl of water decorated with lemon slices on the table, so that your guests can rinse their fingers.

Braised Balinese Duck

I remember this dish, with its wonderful aroma, from my first visit to Bali in the early 1980s. It makes an ideal main course for a special occasion, and once the spice paste has been made, much of the work is done. The lovely savoury spices make a delicious contrast to the rich duck meat, producing a truly memorable feast. It takes a little time, but the end result is worth it! Serve with plain rice.

Step one Preheat the oven to 160°C/325°F/gas 3. If the duck is frozen, thaw it thoroughly. Rinse well and blot it completely dry with kitchen paper.

Step two Peel off the tough outer layers of the lemon grass sticks, leaving the tender, whitish centre. Crush with the flat of a knife, then cut into 7.5cm (3in) pieces. Put the lemon grass in a blender or food-processor with all the remaining spice paste ingredients and blend as smoothly as possible.

Step three Transfer the spice paste to a saucepan and simmer over a low heat for about 5 minutes, until thoroughly cooked, adding more water if the paste begins to stick to the pan.

Step four Now rub the paste over the duck, inside and out. Carefully wrap the duck in several layers of foil, sealing it well. Place the wrapped duck on a rack set over a roasting tin, pour a little water into the tin to prevent the fat splattering, and cook for 1 hour. Then reduce the heat to 140°C/275°F/gas 1 and continue to cook for 2 hours.

Step five Remove the duck from the oven, unwrap it and pour any liquid into a heatproof glass bowl. Allow it to stand for a few minutes, then discard the surface fat, saving the juices. Leave the duck to stand for at least 10 minutes before you carve it. Using a cleaver or a sharp knife, cut the skin and meat into pieces; it should be very tender. Arrange on a warm platter and serve at once, with the juices poured over the pieces.

Serves 4–6

1 x 2.75kg (6lb) duck, fresh or frozen

for the spice paste

2 fresh sticks of lemon grass

4 garlic cloves, peeled

6 shallots, peeled

3 tbsp coarsely chopped fresh galangal or root ginger

6 red chillies, de-seeded

3 tbsp lime juice

2 tsp coriander seeds

2 tsp cumin seeds

2 cloves

1 tsp ground cinnamon

½ tsp grated nutmeg

½ tsp ground turmeric

2 tsp shrimp paste

½ tsp freshly ground black pepper

2 tsp salt

2 tbsp sesame oil

3 tbsp water

Vietnamese Braised Pork

This hearty, savoury dish has some affinities with a Chinese dish from Shanghai, but is simpler to make. Vietnamese cooks use fish sauce instead of soy sauce, which gives a different but equally tasty result. An added bonus is that it reheats extremely well.

Serves 6

about 3 tbsp groundnut oil

1kg (2¼ lb) pork belly, including the rind, cut into 5cm (2in) pieces

6 spring onions, cut into 7.5cm x 5mm (3 x ¼ in) pieces

600ml (1 pint) home-made chicken stock (see page 7) or good-quality bought stock

3 tbsp sugar

1 tsp salt

2 tsp freshly ground black pepper

2 tbsp fish sauce

Step one Heat a wok or large frying pan over a high heat. Add the oil and, when it is very hot and slightly smoking, fry the pieces of pork belly in it until they are crisp and brown all over (cover the wok to prevent splattering). Add more oil if necessary. Remove the pork from the wok and drain well.

Step two Put the spring onions, stock, sugar, salt and pepper into a large casserole and bring to a simmer. Add the browned pork belly and simmer slowly, uncovered, for 1 hour, stirring occasionally. The mixture should become quite dry, but do watch that it doesn't burn.

Step three Stir in the fish sauce and cook for another 5 minutes, then serve.

Braised Sichuan-style Spicy Beancurd

This traditional dish from Sichuan province in China is becoming popular in the West. Bland, but very healthy, beancurd is mixed with spicy, fragrant ingredients to produce a sensational dish that is simply mouthwatering. The essence of this recipe lies with the quality of the seasonings and condiments and the care taken in cooking them just right.

Step one Gently cut the beancurd into 4cm (1½in) cubes.

Step two Heat a wok or large frying pan over a high heat, add the groundnut oil and yellow bean sauce and stir-fry for 30 seconds. Add the soy sauce and salt and stir-fry for 1 minute. Add the chilli powder and stir-fry for another 30 seconds. Then pour in the stock, add the beancurd and simmer for 3 minutes.

Step three Stir in the garlic and the cornflour mixture and cook for 1 minute. Ladle the mixture into a serving bowl, sprinkle over the ground Sichuan peppercorns and serve at once.

Serves 4

450g (1lb) fresh beancurd

1 tbsp groundnut oil

1 tbsp whole yellow bean sauce

1 tbsp dark soy sauce

½ tsp salt

1 tsp red chilli powder or cayenne pepper, or to taste

175ml (6fl oz) home-made chicken stock (see page 7) or good-quality bought stock

2 tbsp coarsely chopped garlic

2 tsp cornflour, mixed with 1 tbsp water

1 tsp finely ground roasted Sichuan peppercorns

Steamed Fish with Garlic, Spring Onion and Ginger

Steaming is a great southern Chinese tradition and is my favourite method of cooking fish, as it preserves the purest flavours of the fish. As it is such a gentle cooking technique, nothing masks the fresh taste of the fish, which remains moist and tender, and you can savour the combination of other ingredients.

Serves 4

450g (1lb) fresh, firm white fish fillets, such as cod, sea bass or turbot

1 tsp coarse sea salt or ordinary cooking salt

1½ tbsp finely shredded fresh root ginger

for the garnish

3 tbsp finely shredded spring onions

1 tbsp light soy sauce

2 tsp dark soy sauce

1 tbsp groundnut oil

2 tsp sesame oil

2 garlic cloves, thinly sliced

Step one Pat the fish fillets or fish dry with kitchen paper. Rub with the salt on both sides, and set aside for 30 minutes. (This helps the flesh to firm up and draws out any excess moisture.)

Step two Set up a steamer, or put a rack into a wok or deep pan and fill with 5cm (2in) of water. Bring the water to the boil over a high heat, then reduce the heat. Put the fish on a heatproof plate and scatter the ginger evenly over the top.

Step three Place the plate in the steamer or on the rack. Cover the pan tightly, and gently steam the fish until just cooked. Flat fish fillets will take about 5 minutes; thicker ones 12–14 minutes.

Step four Remove the plate and fish and sprinkle over the spring onions and soy sauces. Heat the two oils in a small pan and, when they are hot, add the garlic slices and brown them. Pour the garlic oil over the top of the fish and serve.

Three Mushroom Braise

The three mushrooms in this dish have very different characteristics. Straw have a musky scent and meaty texture; Chinese dried are smoky-flavoured and densely textured, while button are mild.

Step one Soak the dried mushrooms in warm water for 20 minutes, then drain. Rinse well and squeeze out any excess liquid. Discard the tough stems, shred the caps and set aside.

Step two Heat a wok or large frying pan over a high heat, add the oil and, when slightly smoking, add the garlic and stir-fry for 15 seconds. Add all the mushrooms and stir-fry, mixing together, for a few seconds. Add the soy sauce, rice wine or dry sherry, oyster sauce, sugar and chicken stock. Reduce the heat and cook, stirring, for 7 minutes until the fresh mushrooms are cooked.

Step three Increase the heat to high and continue to cook until most of the liquid has reduced. Mix in the spring onions and serve.

You can use the soaking water from Chinese dried mushrooms for making soups or cooking rice. Strain the liquid through a fine sieve to discard any sand or residue before using.

Serves 4

25g (1oz) Chinese dried mushrooms (see tip)

1 tbsp groundnut oil

3 garlic cloves, thinly sliced

225g (8oz) tin Chinese straw mushrooms, drained, rinsed and left whole

85g (3oz) button mushrooms, sliced

1 tbsp light soy sauce

2 tbsp Shaoxing rice wine or dry sherry

3 tbsp oyster sauce

2 tsp sugar

75ml (2½ fl oz) home-made chicken stock (see page 7) or good-quality bought stock

2 tbsp finely chopped spring onions

Steamed Scallops with Chilli and Ginger

Fresh scallops are sweet and rich. Perhaps the best way to preserve their qualities is the Chinese technique of steaming. Using hot, wet vapours, this method brings out the succulent texture of scallops without overcooking them.

Serves 4

450g (1lb) fresh scallops, including the corals

2 fresh red chillies, de-seeded and chopped

2 tsp finely chopped fresh root ginger

1 tbsp Shaoxing rice wine or dry sherry

1 tbsp light soy sauce

¼ tsp salt

¼ tsp freshly ground black pepper

3 tbsp finely chopped spring onions

Step one Place the scallops evenly on a round heatproof platter. Then evenly distribute the chillies, ginger, rice wine or dry sherry, soy sauce, salt, pepper and spring onions on top.

Step two Next, set up a steamer or put a rack into a wok or deep pan and fill it with 5cm (2in) of water. Bring the water to the boil over a high heat. Carefully lower the platter of scallops into the steamer or on to the rack. Reduce the heat to low and cover the wok or pan tightly. Steam gently for 5 minutes. Remove and serve at once.

Braised Korean-style Spareribs

Korean food is one of the least known of all Asian cuisines. It is a cuisine that uses many of the same ingredients as Chinese, but combines them in different ways. One delicious dish that I have eaten in Korean restaurants is this one with spareribs. I have added my own touches.

Step one Have your butcher separate the spareribs into individual ribs and then into chunks which are about 7.5cm (3in) long. Alternatively, do this yourself using a heavy, sharp cleaver that can cut through bones.

Step two Heat a wok or large frying pan over a high heat. Add the oil and, when it is very hot and slightly smoking, add the spareribs and stir-fry them for 5 minutes or until they are brown. Remove them with a slotted spoon and discard all the oil and fat. Wipe the wok clean.

Step three Put the rest of the ingredients into the clean wok or frying pan. Bring the mixture to the boil and then reduce the heat. Add the spareribs, cover and simmer slowly for about 45 minutes, stirring occasionally. If necessary, add a little water to the sauce to prevent the dish from drying out. Skim off any surface fat, turn on to a warm serving platter and serve immediately.

Serves 4

750g (1¾lb) meaty pork spareribs

1 tbsp groundnut oil

5 garlic cloves, crushed

1 tbsp finely chopped fresh root ginger

3 tbsp finely chopped spring onions

3 tbsp rock or granulated sugar

3 tbsp Shaoxing rice wine or dry sherry

300ml (10fl oz) home-made chicken stock (see page 7) or good-quality bought stock

2 tbsp light soy sauce

2 tbsp sesame paste or peanut butter

Quick and Healthy Steamed Chicken

Steaming is not only a healthy way to cook food, it also brings out the subtle flavours. By keeping the food moist and cooking it slowly in warm vapours, good chicken comes out even better. Chinese cooks tend to steam the entire chicken, but when I am in a hurry I simply steam the chicken breasts. The result is a quick, but healthy, meal that takes little time to prepare. The juices from the chicken taste delicious over rice.

Serves 4

450g (1lb) skinless, boneless chicken breasts

1 tsp coarse sea salt or ordinary cooking salt

1 tbsp light soy sauce

1 tbsp Shaoxing rice wine or dry sherry

½ tsp freshly ground white pepper

1 egg white

2 tsp cornflour

1 tsp sesame oil

1½ tsp finely shredded fresh root ginger

for the garnish

3 tbsp finely shredded spring onions

1 tbsp groundnut oil

2 tsp sesame oil

Step one Combine the chicken with the salt, soy sauce, rice wine or dry sherry, pepper, egg white, cornflour and sesame oil. Leave to marinate for at least 20 minutes.

Step two Next, set up a steamer or put a rack into a wok or deep pan and fill it with 5cm (2in) of water. Bring the water to the boil over a high heat, then reduce the heat. Put the chicken on a heatproof plate and scatter the ginger evenly over the top. Put the plate in the steamer or on the rack. Cover the pan tightly and gently steam the chicken until it is just white and firm. It will take about 8–10 minutes to cook, depending on the thickness of the breasts.

Step three Remove the plate and chicken and sprinkle over the spring onions. Heat the two oils together in a small pan and, when they are hot, pour the oil mixture over the top of the chicken. Serve at once.

Braised Chicken with Fresh Water Chestnuts

Chicken is best when its mild flavour and soft texture are combined with other distinctive tastes and contrasting textures. Sweet, fresh, crispy water chestnuts are thus an admirable partner in any chicken dish.

Step one If you are using unboned thighs, remove the skin and bones from the chicken thighs or have your butcher do it for you. Cut the chicken into 2.5cm (1in) chunks and combine it in a bowl with the marinade ingredients. Leave to marinate for at least 30 minutes in the fridge.

Step two Heat a wok or large frying pan over a high heat. Add the oil and, when it is very hot and slightly smoking, add the chicken and stir-fry for 5 minutes. Remove and drain the chicken. Now drain off all but 2 teaspoons of the oil from the wok.

Step three Reheat the wok, add the garlic and ginger and stir-fry for 30 seconds. Then add the drained chicken to the wok with all the remaining ingredients. Reduce the heat to low, cover and cook for 10 minutes, stirring from time to time, until the chicken is cooked. Give the mixture a good stir, pour on to a warm platter and serve at once.

Serves 4

450g (1lb) boneless, skinless chicken thighs or 900g (2lb) chicken thighs with bone in

2 tbsp groundnut oil

3 garlic cloves, thinly sliced

1½ tbsp finely shredded fresh root ginger

225g (8oz) water chestnuts

3 tbsp home-made chicken stock (see page 7) or good-quality bought stock

2 tbsp oyster sauce

1 tbsp Shaoxing rice wine or dry sherry

1 tsp dark soy sauce

1 tsp light soy sauce

1 tsp sugar

for the marinade

2 tsp light soy sauce

2 tsp Shaoxing rice wine or dry sherry

1 tsp sesame oil

2 tsp cornflour

Braised Aubergine Casserole with Prawns

Here, in an unlikely combination, I have paired aubergines with prawns.
Their distinctive flavours at once contrast and enhance each other.

Serves 4

450g (1lb) Chinese or
ordinary aubergines

175g (6oz) raw prawns

1½ tbsp groundnut oil

2 tbsp coarsely
chopped garlic

1½ tbsp finely
chopped fresh
root ginger

3 tbsp finely chopped
spring onions, white
part only

1 tbsp dark soy sauce

1 tbsp light soy sauce

1 tbsp chilli
bean sauce

1 tbsp whole yellow
bean sauce

1 tbsp Shaoxing rice
wine or dry sherry

1 tbsp sugar

1 tbsp Chinese
black cider vinegar
or cider vinegar

2 tsp Szechuan
peppercorns, roasted
and ground

300ml (10fl oz)
home-made chicken
stock (see page 7)
or good-quality
bought stock

to garnish

2 tsp sesame oil

2 tbsp chopped green
spring onions

Step one Roll-cut the Chinese aubergines by cutting them at a
slight diagonal slant, rolling them half-way round, then cutting
again. If you are using the large variety, trim and cut them into
2.5cm (1in) cubes, sprinkle them with 2 teaspoons of salt (only
if you are using ordinary aubergines – you do not need to salt
Chinese aubergines) and leave them in a sieve to drain for 20
minutes. Then rinse them under cold running water and pat
them dry with kitchen paper.

Step two Peel the prawns and discard the shells. Using a small
sharp knife, remove the fine digestive cord. Wash the prawns
and pat them dry with kitchen paper. Coarsely chop them and
set aside.

Step three Heat a wok or large frying pan over a high heat.
Add the oil and, when it is very hot and slightly smoking, add
the garlic, ginger and spring onions and stir-fry them for 30
seconds, then add the aubergines and continue to stir-fry for
1 minute. Add the rest of the ingredients, except the prawns.
Reduce the heat and cook, uncovered, for 10–15 minutes until
the aubergines are tender, stirring occasionally.

Step four Return the heat to high and continue to stir until the
liquid has been reduced and has thickened slightly. Add the
prawns and cook for another 2 minutes. Turn the mixture on to
a warm serving dish and garnish with drizzled sesame oil and
the chopped spring onion tops and serve at once.

Braised Garlic Chicken

Braised in this way, the whole garlic becomes mild and sweet. Most of the resulting sauce cooks off, leaving a tender, aromatic chicken dish – and the bonus is that it is quick to make. Serve this dish with potatoes or plain rice and another vegetable dish.

Step one Blot the chicken thighs dry with kitchen paper. Sprinkle them evenly with the salt and pepper, then sprinkle with the flour, shaking off any excess.

Step two Heat a wok or large frying pan over a high heat. Add the oil and, when it is very hot and slightly smoking, reduce the heat to low. Add the chicken, skin-side down, and slowly brown on both sides for about 10 minutes. Drain off all excess fat, add the garlic cloves and stir-fry for 2 minutes. Then add the rice wine or dry sherry, soy sauce and stock or water. Turn the heat as low as possible, cover and braise for 20 minutes until the chicken is tender.

Step three When the chicken and garlic are cooked, remove them from the wok with a slotted spoon and place them on a warm platter. Sprinkle with the chives and serve at once.

Serves 4

900g (2lb) chicken thighs with bone in

2 tsp salt

1 tsp freshly ground black pepper

2 tbsp plain flour

3 tbsp groundnut oil

15 whole garlic cloves, unpeeled

2 tbsp Shaoxing rice wine or dry sherry

1 tbsp light soy sauce

3 tbsp home-made chicken stock (see page 7) or good-quality bought stock, or water

2 tbsp finely snipped fresh chives, to garnish

Stir-fried Curry Beef

Although curry is not a Chinese seasoning, it has nevertheless made its way into Chinese cuisine in a rather mild form. The hint of exotic spices adds a special, very subtle flavour to any Chinese dish. It works extremely well when beef is matched with vegetables. The best type of curry paste or powder to use is the Madras variety, which is the one favoured by most Chinese cooks.

Serves 2–4

450g (1lb) lean beef steak

3 tbsp groundnut oil

225g (8oz) onions, sliced

2 tbsp coarsely chopped garlic

1½ tbsp shredded spring onions, to garnish

for the marinade

1 tbsp light soy sauce

2 tsp sesame oil

1 tbsp Shaoxing rice wine or dry sherry

2 tsp cornflour

for the curry sauce

1 tbsp Shaoxing rice wine or dry sherry

1 tbsp Madras curry paste or powder

1 tbsp dark soy sauce

1 tbsp light soy sauce

1 tsp sugar

2 tbsp home-made chicken stock (see page 7) or good-quality bought stock or water

Step one Cut the beef into slices 5cm (2in) long and 5mm (¼in) thick and put them into a bowl. Add all the marinade ingredients, mix well and leave to marinate for 20 minutes.

Step two Heat a wok or large frying pan over a high heat. Add the groundnut oil and, when it is very hot and slightly smoking, add the beef slices and stir-fry for 3–5 minutes, until lightly browned. Remove and drain well in a colander set inside a bowl.

Step three Wipe the wok or pan clean and reheat it over a high heat. Add 1 tablespoon of the drained oil, then add the onions and garlic and stir-fry for 1 minute.

Step four Add all the ingredients for the curry sauce, bring the mixture to a simmer and cook for 3 minutes. Return the drained beef slices to the wok or pan and toss them thoroughly with the sauce. Turn the mixture on to a warm serving platter, garnish with the spring onions and serve at once.

Beef with Orange

This is a dish from northern and western China. The Chinese always use dried peel – the older the skin, the more prized the flavour. It's easy to make your own dried peel (see page 195), but I have often made this dish with fresh orange peel and find that the tartness works just as well with the robust flavour of the beef. This is an easy dish to make and is a pleasant change of flavour from the usual stir-fried beef recipes.

Step one Cut the beef into thin slices 5cm (2in) long, cutting against the grain. Put the beef into a bowl, add all the marinade ingredients and mix well. Leave to marinate for about 20 minutes.

Step two Heat a wok or large frying pan over a high heat. Add the groundnut oil and, when it is very hot and slightly smoking, remove the beef from the marinade with a slotted spoon. Add the beef to the pan and stir-fry for 3–5 minutes or until browned. Remove and leave to drain in a colander set inside a bowl.

Step three Pour off most of the oil from the wok or pan, leaving about 2 teaspoons. Reheat over a high heat, add the dried chilli peppers and stir-fry for 10 seconds.

Step four Return the beef to the pan, add the rest of the ingredients and stir-fry for 4 minutes, mixing well. Serve at once.

Serves 4

450g (1lb)
lean beef steak

65ml (2½ fl oz)
groundnut oil

2 dried red chilli
peppers, cut in half
lengthways

1 tbsp dried orange
peel, soaked and
coarsely chopped
(see page 195)

2 tsp whole Sichuan
peppercorns, roasted
and finely ground
(optional)

1 tbsp dark soy sauce

½ tsp salt

½ tsp freshly ground
black pepper

1½ tsp sugar

2 tsp sesame oil

for the marinade

1 tbsp dark soy sauce

1 tbsp Shaoxing rice
wine or dry sherry

1½ tbsp finely
chopped fresh
root ginger

2 tsp cornflour

2 tsp sesame oil

Beef with Ginger and Pineapple

This recipe is derived from the original I enjoyed at Yah Toh Heen (the former Lai Ching Heen), the marvellous Chinese restaurant in Hong Kong's InterContinental (formerly the Regent Hotel). I regard it as exemplary of the innovative New Hong Kong Cuisine, in which new ingredients and techniques are being employed to transform traditional recipes. A mouth-watering combination of tastes and textures, it is remarkably easy to prepare. You can, if you wish, prepare the meat, vegetables and fruit in advance and store them, well wrapped, in the fridge until you are ready to cook.

Serves 4–6

450g (1lb) lean beef steak

2 tbsp groundnut oil

2 tbsp finely shredded fresh root ginger

2 red peppers, cut into strips

2 spring onions, cut into 7.5cm (3in) lengths

1 tbsp water

2 tsp Shaoxing rice wine or dry sherry

1 tsp light soy sauce

225g (8oz) piece freshly peeled pineapple, cored and cut into 4–6 thick slices

2 tsp sesame oil

for the marinade

1 tsp salt

2 tsp Shaoxing rice wine or dry sherry

2 tsp sesame oil

1½ tsp cornflour

Step one Cut the beef into slices 5cm (2in) long and 5mm (¼in) thick and put them in a bowl. Add all the marinade ingredients, mix well and leave to marinate for 10 minutes.

Step two Heat a wok or large frying pan over a high heat. Add the groundnut oil and, when it is very hot and slightly smoking, add the beef and stir-fry for 3–5 minutes, or until browned. Remove with a slotted spoon and drain in a colander set inside a bowl.

Step three Add the ginger, red peppers and spring onions to the wok and stir-fry for 1 minute. Pour in the water, the rice wine or sherry and the soy sauce and cook for 3 minutes.

Step four Drain the juices from the beef into the wok and add the pineapple. Return the beef to the wok and cook until it and the pineapple are heated through. Add the sesame oil and give the mixture one or two final stirs. Serve at once.

Sichuan-style Pork with Peanuts

This is a pork version of a classic Sichuan Chinese dish that is usually made with chicken. It is quick and easy to prepare and is quite savoury – as is to be expected from any Sichuan recipe. Serve with plain rice and another vegetable dish for a complete meal.

Step one Cut the pork into 2.5cm (1in) cubes and put them in a bowl. Add all the marinade ingredients, mix well and leave to marinate for 10 minutes.

Step two Heat a wok or large frying pan over a high heat. Add the groundnut oil and, when it is hot and slightly smoking, add the chilli and stir-fry for a few seconds (you may remove it when it turns black or leave it in; leaving it in will make the flavour stronger). Add the peanuts and stir-fry them for 1 minute. Remove the peanuts from the wok and set aside.

Step three Lift the pork from the marinade with a slotted spoon, add to the wok and stir-fry for 3 minutes or until lightly browned. Remove and drain in a colander set inside a bowl.

Step four Wipe the wok clean and add all the sauce ingredients, except the sesame oil. Bring to the boil and then reduce the heat. Return the pork to the wok and cook for about 2 minutes, mixing well all the time.

Step five Finally, return the peanuts to the wok and add the sesame oil. Give the mixture a good stir and serve immediately.

Serves 4

450g (1lb) lean boneless pork

1½ tbsp groundnut oil

1 dried red chilli, split lengthways

6 tbsp raw peanuts

for the marinade

1 tbsp light soy sauce

2 tsp Shaoxing rice wine or dry sherry

1 tsp sesame oil

2 tsp cornflour

for the sauce

2 tbsp home-made chicken stock (see page 7) or good-quality bought stock, or water

2 tbsp Shaoxing rice wine or dry sherry

1 tbsp dark soy sauce

2 tsp sugar

1 tbsp chopped garlic

1½ tbsp finely chopped spring onions

2 tsp finely chopped fresh root ginger

1 tbsp Chinese black rice vinegar or cider vinegar

1 tsp salt

1 tsp sesame oil

...ied Pork with Lychees

In China, pork is almost always served as an accompaniment to non-meat foods. In this recipe it is paired with lychees. Try to use fresh ones: their tangy, grape-like flavour goes nicely with pork, at once complementing and contrasting it. Serve over rice (see page 64).

Serves 4–6

450g (1lb) lean pork

225g (8oz) fresh or tinned lychees

1½ tbsp groundnut oil

2 tbsp coarsely chopped garlic

2 tbsp coarsely chopped spring onions, to garnish

for the marinade

2 tsp light soy sauce

2 tsp Shaoxing rice wine or dry sherry

1 tsp sesame oil

2 tsp cornflour

Step one Cut the pork into slices 5cm (2in) long and 5mm (¼in) thick and put them in a bowl. Add all the marinade ingredients, mix well and leave to marinate for a few minutes.

Step two If you are using fresh lychees, peel them and remove the stones. If you are using tinned lychees, drain off the liquid (which you will not need for this dish).

Step three Heat a wok or large frying pan, add the groundnut oil and garlic and stir-fry for 10 seconds. Put in the pork and continue to stir-fry for about 2 minutes or until it is just cooked through.

Step four Add the lychees and stir-fry for another 30 seconds to warm them through. Garnish with the chopped spring onions and serve at once.

Stir-fried Pork with Spinach

I love this simple dish, which my working mother often used to make. No wonder – it is not only tasty, but healthy as well, and it was the only way she got me to eat spinach. The secret is to cook this dish in two stages: first the meat and then the spinach. This way, the meat does not stew in the spinach juices and become tough.

Step one Wash the spinach thoroughly and remove all the stalks, leaving just the leaves. Set aside.

Step two Slice the pork into 1 x 7.5cm (½ x 3in) strips and put them in a bowl. Add all the marinade ingredients, mix well and leave to marinate for 10 minutes.

Step three Heat a wok or large frying pan over a high heat. Add the groundnut oil and, when it is very hot and slightly smoking, add the pork and stir-fry for 3 minutes, until browned. Drain immediately in a colander set inside a bowl, leaving 1 tablespoon of oil in the wok.

Step four Reheat the wok. Add the garlic, ginger and some salt and pepper and stir-fry for 30 seconds. Then add the spinach and stir-fry for about 2 minutes to coat the spinach leaves thoroughly in the mixture.

Step five When the spinach has wilted to about a third of its original volume, add the sugar, soy sauces and cooked pork. Stir-fry for 2 minutes, then transfer to a serving platter, garnish with the spring onions. Serve at once.

Serves 2–4

675g (1½lb) fresh spinach

450g (1lb) lean pork fillet

3 tbsp groundnut oil

2 tbsp coarsely chopped garlic

1 tbsp finely shredded fresh root ginger

1 tsp sugar

1 tbsp light soy sauce

2 tsp dark soy sauce

salt and freshly ground black pepper

2 tbsp coarsely chopped spring onions, to garnish

for the marinade

2 tsp light soy sauce

1 tsp Shaoxing rice wine or dry sherry

1 tsp sesame oil

2 tsp cornflour

Hunan-style Lamb

Lamb is not a standard item on southern Chinese menus. It is much more common in northern and central China. The prejudice against lamb may be discerned in a southern saying: 'There are 72 ways of cooking lamb; most of them result in something quite unpalatable.' But this is unfair to lamb. As this recipe shows, it lends itself to imaginative uses. The most tender cuts, such as steaks and chops, are best for this dish.

Serves 4

450g (1lb) lean lamb steak or fillet, or boned loin chops

1 tbsp groundnut oil

3 tbsp finely chopped spring onions, white part only

6 garlic cloves, thinly sliced

2 tsp finely shredded fresh root ginger

1 tbsp chilli bean sauce

1½ tbsp hoisin sauce

1 tsp sugar

1 tsp sesame oil

for the marinade

1 tbsp Shaoxing rice wine or dry sherry

2 tsp dark soy sauce

1 tbsp light soy sauce

2 tsp sesame oil

1½ tsp cornflour

Step one Cut the lamb into thin slices and put them into a bowl. Add all the marinade ingredients, mix well and leave to marinate for 20 minutes. Then drain off and reserve the marinade.

Step two Heat a wok or large frying pan over a high heat. Add the groundnut oil and, when it is very hot and slightly smoking, add the marinated lamb pieces with just a little of the reserved marinade. Stir-fry for 2 minutes.

Step three Add the spring onions, garlic and ginger and stir-fry for another 2 minutes. Add the chilli bean sauce, hoisin sauce and sugar and continue to stir-fry for 2 minutes. Stir in the sesame oil, turn the mixture on to a warm serving platter and serve immediately.

Lamb with Garlic

Lamb is especially delicious when it is stir-fried. This way of preparing it with a lot of garlic and spring onions to balance its strong taste is a popular one. The most tender cuts of lamb, such as steaks or chops, are best for this dish. Serve with rice (see page 64).

Step one Cut the lamb into thin slices and put it in a bowl. Mix in all the marinade ingredients and leave to marinate for 20 minutes. Then drain off the marinade and set the lamb aside.

Step two Heat a wok or large frying pan until it is very hot. Add the groundnut oil and, when it is very hot and slightly smoking, add the marinated lamb pieces with just a little of the marinade. Stir-fry for 2 minutes.

Step three Add the spring onions, garlic and ginger and stir-fry for another 4 minutes. Turn on to a warm serving platter, sprinkle with the ground peppercorns and serve at once.

Serves 4

450g (1lb) lean lamb steak or fillet, or boned loin chops

1 tbsp groundnut oil

2 spring onions, white part only, finely chopped

6 garlic cloves, thinly sliced

2 tsp finely chopped fresh root ginger

1 tsp Sichuan peppercorns, roasted and freshly ground

for the marinade

1 tbsp Shaoxing rice wine or dry sherry

2 tsp dark soy sauce

1 tbsp light soy sauce

2 tsp sesame oil

1½ tsp cornflour

Hot and Tangy Minced Lamb

This dish, in which the flavours of East and West meet, readily combines with pasta, rice, noodles or even bread to make an easy and substantial meal in less than 30 minutes. You can use minced beef instead of lamb, if you prefer. Sesame paste is a rich, thick, creamy brown paste made from roasted sesame seeds and should not be confused with the Middle Eastern tahini. If you cannot find sesame paste, use smooth peanut butter.

Serves 4–6

1 tbsp groundnut oil

450g (1lb) minced lamb

3 tbsp coarsely chopped garlic

2 tbsp coarsely chopped fresh root ginger

2 tbsp tomato paste

2 tbsp sesame paste

1½ tbsp dark soy sauce

1 tbsp lemon juice

1 tbsp chilli bean sauce

2 tsp sugar

1 tbsp Shaoxing rice wine or dry sherry

Step one Heat a wok or large frying pan until very hot, then add the oil and lamb. Stir-fry for 2 minutes, then add the garlic and ginger and cook for another minute.

Step two Stir in the tomato paste, sesame paste, soy sauce, lemon juice, chilli bean sauce, sugar and rice wine or sherry. Cook for 4 minutes, then serve.

You will find it quicker if, as in this recipe, you are required to add a number of ingredients at the same time, you measure them together into a bowl and add them all at once.

Garlic Chicken with Cucumber

Cucumbers are rarely served raw in China; they are delicious cooked. In this recipe they are stir-fried with delicate chicken breasts and flavoured with garlic and chilli.

Step one Peel the cucumber, halve it lengthways and remove the seeds with a teaspoon. Then cut it into 2.5cm (1in) cubes, sprinkle with the salt and leave in a colander to drain for 20 minutes (this removes excess moisture). Rinse the cucumber cubes in cold running water and blot them dry with kitchen paper.

Step two Heat a wok or large frying pan until it is very hot. Add the groundnut oil and, when it is very hot and slightly smoking, add the chicken and stir-fry for a few seconds.

Step three Add all the remaining ingredients, except the cucumber, and stir-fry for 2 minutes. Now add the cucumber cubes and stir-fry for another 3 minutes. Serve at once.

Serves 4

450g (1lb) cucumber (about 2)

2 tsp salt

1 tbsp groundnut oil

450g (1lb) boneless, skinless chicken breasts, cut into 2.5cm (1in) cubes

1½ tbsp finely chopped garlic

1 tbsp finely chopped spring onions

1 tbsp light soy sauce

1 tbsp Shaoxing rice wine or dry sherry

2 tsp chilli bean sauce or chilli powder

2 tsp sesame oil

For a video masterclass on chopping vegetables, go to
www.mykitchentable.co.uk/videos/choppingvegetables

Spicy Chicken with Mint

Here is a lovely, spicy chicken dish with fresh mint as a counterbalance. If you grow your own mint, it is likely to be even more delicate and subtle than anything you can buy. The chicken is 'velveted' to preserve its succulence and flavour. You can use the traditional oil method or, for a less fattening version, substitute water.

Serves 4

450g (1lb) boneless, skinless chicken breasts

300ml (10fl oz) groundnut oil or water, plus 1 tbsp

225g (8oz) red or green peppers, cut into 2.5cm (1in) dice

1 tbsp thinly sliced garlic

150ml (¼ pint) home-made chicken stock (see page 7) or good-quality bought stock

1½ tbsp Madras curry paste

2 tsp chilli bean sauce

2 tsp sugar

1½ tbsp Shaoxing rice wine or dry sherry

1 tbsp light soy sauce

1 tsp cornflour, blended with 1 tbsp water

8 fresh mint leaves

for the marinade

1 egg white

1 tsp salt

2 tsp cornflour

Step one Cut the chicken breasts into 2.5cm (1in) cubes. Mix with all the marinade ingredients in a bowl and refrigerate for 20 minutes.

Step two If cooking the chicken in groundnut oil, heat a wok or frying pan over a high heat and add the oil. When it is very hot, remove the wok from the heat and immediately add the chicken pieces, stirring vigorously to prevent them sticking. After about 2 minutes, when the chicken pieces turn white, quickly drain them in a stainless-steel colander set inside a bowl. Discard the oil. If you use water instead of oil, bring it to the boil in a saucepan, then remove from the heat and immediately add the chicken pieces, stirring vigorously to prevent them sticking. After about 2 minutes, when the chicken pieces turn white, quickly drain them in a colander set inside a bowl. Discard the water.

Step three If you used a wok or pan, wipe it clean. Heat it over a high heat, then add the tablespoon of oil and, when it is very hot and slightly smoking, add the peppers and garlic and stir-fry for 2 minutes.

Step four Add all the remaining ingredients, except the cornflour mixture and mint leaves, and cook for 2 minutes. Add the cornflour mixture and cook for 20 seconds, stirring, then add the drained chicken and stir-fry for another 2 minutes, coating the chicken thoroughly with the sauce. Finally, add the mint leaves and stir for 1 minute to mix well. Turn on to a warm platter and serve at once.

Smoked Chicken

Smoked chicken and duck are very popular in China. Such delicacies require a time-consuming smoking process that, fortunately, is done for us. They are readily available in supermarkets and Chinese grocers, thus making this northern Chinese favourite both appetising and easy to make. Serve with rice (see page 64) and a salad.

Step one With your fingers, tear the meat from the bones of the chicken. Cut it into large shreds and set aside.

Step two Heat a wok or large frying pan over a high heat, and add the groundnut oil, garlic and ginger. Stir-fry for 10 seconds, then add the Chinese leaves and stir-fry for 5 minutes.

Step three Add the soy sauce and rice wine or sherry and cook for another minute. Then add the smoked chicken and heat through. Serve at once.

Serves 4–6

675g (1½ lb) smoked chicken

1½ tbsp groundnut oil

3 tbsp chopped garlic

1 tbsp coarsely chopped fresh root ginger

450g (1lb) Chinese leaves (Peking cabbage), coarsely chopped

1 tbsp dark soy sauce

1 tbsp Shaoxing rice wine or dry sherry

Chicken Livers with Onions

Chicken livers are among the easiest foods to prepare. The trick is to combine them with the proper seasonings and spices, so that their delicacy is retained, but they are also given a new dimension. Hence the onions and the five-spice powder in this recipe – and it works! Serve this dish as part of a Chinese meal or as a main course with rice (see page 64) and a vegetable. Calves' liver may be substituted for the chicken livers if you wish.

Serves 2–4

450g (1lb) chicken livers, cut into bite-sized pieces

5 tsp Shaoxing rice wine or dry sherry

1 tbsp light soy sauce

½ tsp five-spice powder

1 tsp salt

¼ tsp freshly ground black pepper

1 tbsp cornflour

5 tsp groundnut oil

2 onions, sliced

2 tsp sesame oil

Step one Combine the chicken livers with 3 teaspoons of the rice wine or sherry, the soy sauce, five-spice powder, ½ teaspoon of the salt, the pepper and cornflour. Mix well.

Step two Heat a wok or large frying pan over a high heat, then add 2 teaspoons of the groundnut oil. Add the livers and stir-fry for about 4 minutes, until they are brown on the outside, but still pink inside. Remove the livers from the wok.

Step three Wipe the wok clean, then reheat. Add the remaining oil, the remaining salt and the onions. Stir-fry for 4 minutes or until the onions are brown and slightly caramelised. Return the livers to the wok and add the remaining 2 teaspoons of rice wine or sherry and the sesame oil. Stir-fry for 2 minutes, then serve at once.

For a video masterclass on how to chop an onion, go to
www.mykitchentable.co.uk/videos/choppingonion

Hot Pepper Prawns

I was introduced to this dish one evening when I dined with Madhur Jaffrey and her husband at the Shun Lee Palace restaurant in New York. She suggested that I try it, predicting that I would appreciate the imaginative interplay of pungent aromas and spicy flavours. How right she was. This is an exciting treat for the taste buds and very easy to prepare. Serve it with rice (see page 64). For a one-dish meal, double the quantity of sauce and toss the sauce and prawns with fresh egg noodles or rice noodles.

Step one Peel the prawns, make a slit down the back of each one and pull out the fine digestive cord with the tip of the knife. Wash the prawns in cold water with 1 tablespoon of salt, then drain and repeat. Rinse well and pat dry with kitchen paper.

Step two Combine the prawns with the teaspoon of salt, plus the cornflour and sesame oil and mix well.

Step three Heat a wok or large frying pan over a high heat and add the groundnut oil and prawns. Stir-fry for 1 minute, then remove the prawns with a slotted spoon. Add the chillies, black beans, garlic and spring onions to the wok and stir-fry for 20 seconds.

Step four Add the vinegar, soy sauce and sugar. Stir in the cornflour mixture and return the prawns to the wok. Cook for another 2 minutes, then serve at once.

Serves 4

450g (1lb) raw prawns

1 tbsp salt, plus 1 tsp

2 tsp cornflour

2 tsp sesame oil

2 tbsp groundnut oil

2 fresh chillies, de-seeded and coarsely chopped

1 tbsp salted black beans

2 tbsp coarsely chopped garlic

4 tbsp coarsely chopped spring onions

3 tbsp white rice vinegar

2 tbsp dark soy sauce

1 tbsp sugar

2 tsp cornflour, blended with 2 tsp water

Prawn and Pork Stir-fry

The Chinese combine foods in an unusual way, sometimes mixing seafood with meats, especially pork. The result is delicious, savoury and very tasty. Here, minced pork is used to extend the more expensive prawns. This recipe is equally good made with fresh scallops.

Serves 4

225g (8oz) raw prawns

2 tbsp salt

450ml (15fl oz) groundnut oil or water

1 tbsp groundnut oil

2 tbsp coarsely chopped salted black beans

1½ tbsp finely chopped fresh root ginger

2 tsp finely chopped garlic

450g (1lb) minced pork

1 tbsp dark soy sauce

2 tsp light soy sauce

1 tbsp Shaoxing rice wine or dry sherry

salt and freshly ground white pepper

½ tsp sugar

2 tsp sesame oil

2 tbsp finely chopped spring onions, to garnish

for the marinade

1 egg white

2 tsp cornflour

1 tsp sesame oil

salt and freshly ground white pepper

Step one Peel the prawns, make a slit down the back of each one and pull out the fine digestive cord with the tip of the knife. Wash the prawns in cold water with 1 tablespoon of salt, then drain and repeat. Rinse well and pat dry with kitchen paper.

Step two Combine the prawns with all the marinade ingredients, mix well and leave in the fridge for 20 minutes.

Step three If using groundnut oil to cook the prawns, heat a wok or large frying pan over a high heat and add the oil. When it is very hot, remove the wok or pan from the heat and immediately add the prawns, stirring vigorously to prevent them sticking. After about 2 minutes, when they turn white, quickly drain the prawns in a stainless-steel colander set inside a bowl. Discard the oil. If you use water instead of oil, bring it to the boil in a saucepan, then remove from the heat and immediately add the prawns, stirring vigorously to prevent them sticking. After about 2 minutes, when the prawns turn white, quickly drain them in a colander set inside a bowl. Discard the water.

Step four If you used a wok or pan, wipe it clean. Heat it over a high heat, then add the tablespoon of oil and, when it is very hot and slightly smoking, add the black beans, ginger and garlic and stir-fry for 10 seconds.

Step five Add the pork and continue to stir-fry for 5 minutes. Drain the pork of any excess oil. Add the prawns to the wok, together with the soy sauces, rice wine or sherry, salt, pepper and sugar. Stir-fry the mixture for 1 minute, then stir in the sesame oil. Turn on to a warm platter, garnish with the spring onions and serve at once.

Spicy Salmon

Fresh salmon is a quick fish to cook. Its rich, fatty flesh makes it an ideal foil for spices. Of course, it is important to get the highest-quality salmon you can afford, organic if possible. Lightly pan-fried in a hot wok, it makes a fast and wholesome meal.

Step one Lay the salmon fillets on a platter. Put all the spices in a small bowl and mix well. Sprinkle the spice mixture evenly on both sides of the salmon fillets.

Step two Heat a wok or frying pan over a high heat. Add the oil and, when the oil is hot and slightly smoking, add the salmon fillets and sear on one side for 3–4 minutes. Turn over and sear the other side for another 3–4 minutes. Transfer the salmon to a warm platter. Garnish with the spring onions and serve at once.

Serves 4

4 thick-cut boneless salmon fillets, each weighing about 100g (4oz), skinned

3 tbsp groundnut oil

3 tbsp finely chopped spring onions, to garnish

for the spice mix

1 tsp salt

1 tsp freshly ground black pepper

2 tsp chilli powder

1 tsp five-spice powder

½ tsp ground cumin

½ tsp ground coriander

1 tsp sugar

For a video masterclass on filleting salmon, go to
www.mykitchentable.co.uk/videos/filleting

KITCHEN
TABLE

Spicy Courgettes

Courgettes lend themselves to stir-frying in the wok, especially with spices. This dish is not only healthy, but will easily satisfy anyone with a craving for a tasty vegetarian meal. It also makes a lovely accompaniment to a main course.

Serves 4–6

2 tbsp groundnut oil

3 tbsp coarsely chopped garlic

675g (1½lb) (4 medium) courgettes, quartered lengthways and thickly sliced

2 tbsp chilli bean sauce

1 tbsp dark soy sauce

2 tsp light soy sauce

1 tbsp Shaoxing rice wine or dry sherry

3 tbsp water

salt and freshly ground black pepper

2 tsp sesame oil

Step one Heat a wok or large frying pan over a high heat. Add the groundnut oil and, when it is hot, add the garlic and stir-fry for 30 seconds. Then add the courgettes and stir-fry for 2 minutes.

Step two Add the chilli bean sauce, soy sauces, rice wine or sherry, water and some salt and pepper. Cover and cook for 3–5 minutes, until the courgettes are tender. If the wok is dry, add another tablespoon of water. When the courgettes are tender, stir in the sesame oil and serve at once.

Hot and Spicy Stir-fried Cabbage

Cabbage has a distinctive but delicate flavour that adapts well to a wide range of seasonings. Because it is a 'cold' vegetable, I believe it needs the assistance or enhancement of something like zesty Sichuan spices, as in this recipe. This dish makes a delicious accompaniment to all types of main course. With rice and another quick vegetable dish, it may also serve as part of a vegetarian meal. You can use Chinese leaves (Peking cabbage) instead of cabbage, if you wish.

Step one Bring a large pan of salted water to the boil, add the cabbage and blanch for 2 minutes – this removes any harshness of flavour and brings out the sweet taste. Drain thoroughly.

Step two Heat a wok or large frying pan over a high heat, then add the oil, garlic and ginger and stir-fry for about 10 seconds.

Step three Add the cabbage and stir-fry for 2 minutes. Add the sauces and sesame oil and cook for another 2 minutes. Serve at once.

Serves 4–6

450g (1lb) cabbage, cut into strips about 1cm (½ in) wide

1½ tbsp groundnut oil

2 tbsp coarsely chopped garlic

1 tbsp coarsely chopped fresh root ginger

1 tbsp dark soy sauce

1 tbsp oyster sauce

2 tsp chilli bean sauce

2 tsp sesame oil

Eggs and Corn with Spring Onions and Ginger

I often make this dish when I am hungry and need a sustaining, nutritious meal in a hurry. Corn has made its way from the West to China, and in Hong Kong especially you will find it a popular food. You can substitute fresh or frozen peas for the corn, if you wish.

Serves 4

450g (1lb) corn on the cob or 275g (10oz) frozen sweetcorn

1 tbsp groundnut oil

3 tbsp coarsely chopped spring onions

2 tsp finely chopped fresh root ginger

1 tsp salt

4 eggs, lightly beaten

Step one If using corn on the cob, strip off the husks and the silk and cut off the kernels with a sharp knife or cleaver. You should end up with about 275g (10oz). If you are using frozen corn, place it in a bowl and let it thaw at room temperature.

Step two Heat a wok or large frying pan over a high heat. Add the oil and, when it is slightly smoking, add the spring onions, ginger and salt and stir-fry for 10 seconds. Add the corn and stir-fry for 2 minutes.

Step three Finally, reduce the heat to medium, add the eggs and continue to cook for 2 minutes. Serve at once.

Quick Curry Noodles

Chinese noodles are perfect for a quick, tasty meal. In this recipe, the noodles are tossed in an unusual East–West sauce of mustard, curry and soy. The bold flavours marry well with the bland noodles.

Step one Cook the noodles in a large pan of boiling water for 3–5 minutes, then drain and plunge into cold water. Drain thoroughly and toss them in the sesame oil. (They can be kept in this state, tightly covered with clingfilm, for up to 2 hours in the fridge.)

Step two Heat a wok or large frying pan and add the olive and sesame oils. Immediately, add the shallots and stir-fry for 2 minutes, until lightly browned. Then add the mustard, curry powder, soy sauces and some salt and pepper.

Step three Toss in the cooked noodles and stir-fry for about 3 minutes, until heated through, mixing well all the while. Add the chives, mix well and serve at once.

Serves 4

350g (12oz) dried or fresh Chinese noodles

2 tsp sesame oil

3 tbsp finely chopped fresh chives

for the sauce

3 tbsp extra-virgin olive oil

2 tsp sesame oil

3 tbsp finely chopped shallots

2 tbsp Dijon mustard

1 tbsp Madras curry powder

2 tbsp light soy sauce

1 tbsp dark soy sauce

salt and freshly ground black pepper

alinese-style Crispy Fish

One of the culinary delights of visiting Bali is their wonderful array of fish dishes. Here is a simple one that I love. It is quick and easy to make, but embodies all the tastes of the tropics. Once the sauce is made, all that is left to do is fry the fish, which takes literally minutes.

Serves 2–4

1 tsp salt

½ tsp freshly ground black pepper

450g (1lb) white flat fish fillets, such as Dover sole or plaice, skinned

cornflour for dusting

6 tbsp groundnut oil

for the sauce

2 tbsp groundnut oil

2 onions, finely chopped

3 tbsp finely chopped garlic

2 tsp finely chopped fresh ginger

1 tsp grated lemon zest

1 tsp salt

1 tbsp dark soy sauce

2 tbsp lemon juice

freshly ground black pepper

Step one To make the sauce, heat a wok or large frying pan over a high heat. Add the oil and, when it is very hot and slightly smoking, add the onions. Stir-fry for 5 minutes or until they are soft and translucent. Add the garlic, ginger, lemon zest, salt, soy sauce, lemon juice and some black pepper. Reduce the heat to low and simmer for 2 minutes, then set aside.

Step two Sprinkle the salt and pepper evenly over the fish fillets and dust them with cornflour, shaking off any excess.

Step three You will need to cook the fish in 2 batches. Heat a wok, add half the oil and, when it is very hot, add half the fish. Fry for 2 minutes, until it is crisp and brown underneath. Turn over and brown the other side. Remove the fish and drain on kitchen paper, then transfer to a warm platter. Repeat with the remaining oil and fish. Spoon the sauce over the fish and serve at once.

Crispy Vietnamese Prawns

This simple but tasty recipe makes a delightful starter or main course.

Step one Combine the prawns, fish sauce, garlic and black pepper in a bowl and leave to marinate for 1 hour.

Step two In a bowl, combine all the ingredients for the batter. Mix until smooth, then cover and leave to stand for 1 hour.

Step three In a small saucepan, combine all the ingredients for the sweet and spicy dipping sauce, except the cornflour mixture. Bring to the boil, stir in the cornflour mixture and simmer for 1 minute. Remove from the heat and leave to cool.

Step four Dust the prawns with cornflour, shaking off any excess. Heat a wok or deep-fat fryer. Add the oil and, when it is very hot and slightly smoking, dip a handful of prawns into the batter and deep-fry them for 3 minutes, until crisp and golden. If the oil gets too hot, reduce the heat slightly. Drain the prawns well on kitchen paper and then fry the remaining prawns in the same way. Serve immediately, with the sweet and spicy dipping sauce.

Serves 4

450g (1lb) raw prawns, shelled and de-veined, tails on

1 tbsp fish sauce

3 tbsp finely chopped garlic

½ tsp freshly ground black pepper

cornflour for dusting

600ml (1 pint) groundnut or vegetable oil for deep-frying

for the batter

150g (5oz) plain flour

2 tbsp baking powder

1 tsp sugar

½ tsp ground turmeric

½ tsp salt

300ml (10fl oz) water

for the sweet and spicy dipping sauce

150ml (5fl oz) water

3 tbsp sugar

3 tbsp Chinese white rice vinegar or cider vinegar

3 tbsp tomato purée or tomato ketchup

2 tsp chilli bean sauce

1 tsp salt

½ tsp freshly ground white pepper

1 tsp cornflour, mixed with 2 tsp water

143

Singapore-style Oyster Omelette

This recipe is derived from the ones made by Singapore fish hawkers, which is how I learned how easy it is to make. Sweet potato flour gives the dish a delightful, slightly chewy texture and quite an unusual flavour. It may be obtained at a Chinese grocer's, but if you cannot find it, plain flour can be substituted at a pinch. Serve this omelette as a main course or as a starter for a special meal. It is delicious, flavoursome and satisfying.

Serves 4

12 oysters

100g (4oz) sweet potato flour or plain flour

450ml (15fl oz) water

2 tsp salt

2 tsp Shaoxing rice wine or dry sherry

4 eggs, beaten

2 tbsp groundnut oil

3 tbsp finely chopped garlic

3 tbsp finely chopped spring onions

1½ tbsp chilli bean sauce

Step one To open the oysters, cover one hand with a thick cloth and hold an oyster in it. Using a short, sharp, heavy knife in the other hand, prise the shell open next to the hinge. Cut the muscle to loosen the oyster from the shell. Tip the oyster and its juices into a colander set over a bowl. Repeat with the remaining oysters, reserving the juices. Pat the oysters dry with kitchen paper and set aside.

Step two Make a batter by mixing the sweet potato flour with the water, salt, rice wine or sherry and the reserved oyster juices, then beat in the eggs until smooth.

Step three Heat a wok or large frying pan over a high heat. Add the oil and, when it is very hot and slightly smoking, pour in the egg mixture. Stir quickly for 30 seconds, then add the garlic, spring onions, chilli bean sauce and oysters and stir-fry for 1 minute.

Step four Reduce the heat and cook for another 3 minutes, until the egg has set. Serve at once, cut into wedges.

Thai Fishcakes

Nothing could be more tempting than these delicious fishcakes.

Step one To make the cucumber salad, peel the cucumbers and slice them in half lengthways, then use a teaspoon to scrape out the seeds. Cut the cucumber halves into thin slices. In a large bowl, combine the fish sauce or soy sauce, lime juice, water and sugar and stir until the sugar has dissolved. Add the cucumber, chilli and shallots and mix well. Leave to stand for at least 20 minutes before serving.

Step two Cut the fish fillets into pieces about 2.5cm (1in) square. Put the fish, eggs, white pepper and curry paste in a food-processor and blend to a smooth paste (if you use a blender, pulse by turning it on and off until the mixture is combined, otherwise the paste will be rubbery).

Step three Scrape the mixture into a large bowl and fold in the shredded lime leaves or zest, fish sauce, cornflour, sugar, coriander and green beans. On a floured surface, shape the mixture into round, flat patties about 6cm (2½in) in diameter, using a palette knife.

Step four Heat a wok or large frying pan over a high heat. Add the oil and, when it is very hot and slightly smoking, add a handful of the fish cakes and deep-fry for 3 minutes, until golden and crisp. If the oil gets too hot, reduce the heat slightly. Drain the fish cakes well on kitchen paper and keep warm while you fry the remaining ones. Serve immediately, with the cucumber salad.

Serves 4

450g (1lb) skinless, white fish fillet, such as cod, sea bass or halibut

2 eggs, beaten

½ tsp freshly ground white pepper

1 tbsp Thai red curry paste

3 kaffir lime leaves, shredded, or 2 tbsp chopped lime zest

2 tbsp fish sauce (nam pla)

1 tbsp cornflour

2 tsp sugar

2 tbsp chopped fresh coriander

50g (2oz) green beans, chopped

450ml (15fl oz) groundnut oil, for deep-frying

flour, for rolling

for the salad

450g (1lb) cucumbers

3 tbsp fish sauce (nam pla) or light soy sauce

3 tbsp lime juice

3 tbsp water

2 tbsp sugar

1 large, fresh red chilli, de-seeded and finely sliced

3 tbsp finely sliced shallots

Coconut Mussels

Thais love any food from the sea, and no wonder: seafood dishes are easy to prepare, and if you add exotic Thai seasonings, they become a delicious treat. What could be simpler than this recipe made with mussels? You will find this dish, known as *hoy malaeng pooh gathi*, a satisfying fish course that cooks up in minutes – ideal for a crowd.

Serves 4–6

1.5kg (3lb) fresh mussels

2 fresh sticks of lemon grass

1 x 400ml (14fl oz) tin coconut milk

3 tbsp water

3 kaffir lime leaves or 1 tbsp shredded lime zest

2 tbsp coarsely chopped spring onions

1 tbsp Thai green curry paste

3 tbsp chopped coriander roots or stalks

2 tbsp fish sauce (nam pla)

1 tsp sugar

a large handful of fresh Thai basil leaves or ordinary basil leaves, shredded

Step one Scrub the mussels under cold running water and scrape off any barnacles with a small knife. Pull out and discard the fibrous 'beards'. Discard any open mussels that don't close when tapped lightly on a worktop.

Step two Peel off the tough outer layers of the lemon grass sticks, leaving the tender whitish centre. Cut it into 7.5cm (3in) pieces and crush with the flat of a heavy knife.

Step three Pour the coconut milk and water into a wok or large frying pan. Add the lemon grass, lime leaves or zest, spring onions, curry paste, coriander roots or stalks, fish sauce and sugar and bring to a simmer. Add the mussels, then cover and cook over a high heat for 5 minutes, until all the mussels have opened (discard any that remain closed). Give the mixture a final stir, add the basil leaves and serve at once.

Thai Barbecue Chicken

The streets of Thailand are redolent with the aromas of smoky grilled foods. One of the most popular dishes is *gai yang*, a tasty version of barbecue chicken. It is made using chicken thighs, which are not only meatier than breasts, but tend to stay moist despite the intense heat of the grill. The secret is to marinate the chicken overnight if you have the time to do so. Once that is done, the rest is quite easy. It makes a memorable picnic dish or summer meal, served at room temperature.

Step one Put all the marinade ingredients in a blender and process to a smooth purée.

Step two Blot the chicken thighs dry on kitchen paper. Put them in a large bowl, add the marinade and mix well. Cover with clingfilm and leave to marinate in the fridge overnight. The next day, remove the chicken from the fridge and leave at room temperature for 40 minutes before cooking.

Step three Light a barbecue or preheat the grill to high. When the charcoal is ash white or the grill is very hot, grill the thighs for 10 minutes on each side or until cooked through. Place on a warm platter, garnish with the coriander sprigs and serve immediately, or allow to cool and serve at room temperature.

Serves 4

900g (2lb) chicken thighs, with bone in

a handful of fresh coriander sprigs, to garnish

for the marinade

2 tbsp fish sauce (nam pla)

3 tbsp coarsely chopped garlic

3 tbsp chopped fresh coriander

2 small, fresh Thai red or green chillies, de-seeded and chopped

4 kaffir lime leaves or 1 tbsp lime zest

2 tsp sugar

1 tbsp Shaoxing rice wine or dry sherry

1 tsp ground turmeric

2 tsp Thai red curry paste

1 tsp salt

½ tsp freshly ground black pepper

4 tbsp tinned coconut milk

For a video masterclass on on how to tell if your chicken is cooked, go to www.mykitchentable.co.uk/videos/cookingchicken

KITCHEN TABLE

Chicken in Pandan Leaves

This is a version of one of my favourite Thai recipes, *gai hor bai toey*. The chicken is marinated, then wrapped in fragrant pandan leaves and fried, which releases the nut-like flavour of the leaves.

Serves 4–6

450g (1lb) boneless, skinless chicken thighs

40 pandan leaves, cut into 12.5cm (5in) squares

600ml (1 pint) vegetable oil for deep-frying

for the marinade

2 tbsp light soy sauce

3 tbsp coarsely chopped garlic

2 tbsp oyster sauce

2 tsp sugar

2 tbsp finely chopped coriander root or fresh coriander

1 tbsp fish sauce (nam pla)

2 tsp sesame oil

½ tsp freshly ground black pepper

for the sauce

25ml (1fl oz) white rice vinegar or cider vinegar

2 tbsp dark soy sauce

2 tsp sugar

2 tsp roasted sesame seeds

1 small, fresh red Thai chilli, de-seeded and finely chopped

Step one Put all the marinade ingredients in a blender and process to a smooth purée.

Step two Cut the chicken into bite-sized pieces. Put them in a large bowl, add the marinade and mix well. Cover with clingfilm and leave to marinate in the fridge overnight.

Step three When you are ready to cook the chicken, remove it from the fridge and wrap a piece in each pandan leaf (or in a foil square). If your pandan leaves are small, you may have to use more than one, overlapping each other. Tie each parcel with string or secure with bamboo skewers.

Step four Put all the ingredients for the sauce in a bowl and whisk them together, then set aside.

Step five Heat a wok or large, deep frying pan over a very high heat. Add the vegetable oil and, when it is hot and slightly smoking, add the chicken parcels, five at a time, and fry for about 4 minutes, until cooked through. Drain thoroughly on kitchen paper and keep warm while you fry the remaining parcels. Serve immediately, with the sauce.

Indonesian-style Grilled Spicy Chicken

I remember the first time I saw this aromatic chicken dish being cooked on the streets of Jakarta. There, a small whole chicken is marinated and then slowly grilled. The smoky flavours, combined with the spices, were intoxicating. I find using chicken thighs works just as well. It makes a wonderful summer treat and can be served hot or at room temperature.

Step one Put all the marinade ingredients in a blender and process to a smooth purée.

Step two Blot the chicken thighs dry on kitchen paper. Put them in a large bowl, add the marinade and mix well. Cover with clingfilm and leave to marinate in the fridge overnight. The next day, remove the chicken from the fridge and leave at room temperature for 40 minutes.

Step three Light a barbecue or preheat a ridged chargrill pan or the grill. When the charcoal is ash white or the grill is very hot, grill the chicken pieces for 10 minutes on each side or until they are cooked through. Place on a warm platter and serve immediately or allow to cool and serve at room temperature.

Serves 4

900g (2lb) chicken thighs, with bone in

for the marinade

6 tbsp finely chopped shallots

3 tbsp coarsely chopped garlic

3 tbsp finely grated lime or lemon zest

3 fresh red or green chillies, de-seeded and chopped

4 kaffir lime leaves, crushed, or 1 tbsp finely grated lime zest

2 tsp finely chopped fresh ginger

1 tsp ground turmeric

2 tsp ground coriander

1 tsp salt

1 tsp freshly ground black pepper

5 tbsp tinned coconut milk

Crispy Indonesian Chicken

This Javanese-style fried chicken, known as *ayam goreng jawa*, is so popular in Indonesia that some restaurants serve nothing else. I can remember the first time I ate it, outside Jakarta, and how delicious it was. The chicken is cooked in a savoury liquid, then deep-fried until crisp. Nothing could be tastier. The cooking can be done in advance and the deep-frying at the last moment when you are ready to serve the chicken. Plain rice and a salad make splendid accompaniments to this fine dish.

Serves 4

400ml (14fl oz) tinned coconut milk

900g (2lb) chicken thighs, with bone in

600ml (1 pint) groundnut or vegetable oil for deep-frying

for the paste

1 fresh stick of lemon grass

1 tsp finely chopped fresh ginger

1 tsp freshly ground black pepper

2 tbsp crushed garlic

3 fresh red chillies, de-seeded

3 brazil nuts, shelled

2 tsp ground coriander

1 tsp salt

3 shallots, peeled

½ tsp ground turmeric

1 tsp sugar

Step one To make the paste, peel off the tough outer layers of the lemon grass stick, leaving the tender, whitish centre. Crush it with the flat of a knife, then chop finely. Place the lemon grass in a food-processor with all the other paste ingredients, add half the coconut milk and blend until smooth. Pour this mixture into a large saucepan, together with the remaining coconut milk.

Step two Blot the chicken thighs dry on kitchen paper and add to the pan. Bring to a simmer, reduce the heat to as low as possible, then cover and braise for 20 minutes.

Step three Remove the chicken from the pan and leave to cool completely. The chicken can be cooked in advance to this point. When you are ready to serve the dish, heat a wok or deep frying pan over a high heat. Add the groundnut oil and, when it is very hot and slightly smoking, deep-fry the chicken, a few pieces at a time, until crisp and golden. Drain on kitchen paper, then serve at once.

Ten-minute Salmon with Spring Onion Sauce

We Chinese prefer no more than a few hours to elapse between the catching and cooking of fish. Indeed, in many markets in southern China and Hong Kong, fish are sold live. You can select the fish of your choice while it swims around in special glass tanks and then take it home or to a restaurant to be cooked. Serve this truly quick and elegant dish as part of a main course, accompanied by an easy vegetable dish and rice, or as a starter. Sea bass or plaice fillets can be substituted.

Serves 4

450g (1lb) fresh salmon fillets

2 tsp salt

½ tsp freshly ground white or black pepper

for the sauce

6 tbsp coarsely chopped spring onions

1 tbsp finely chopped fresh root ginger (see tip)

1½ tbsp groundnut oil

2 tsp sesame oil

Step one Rub the salmon fillets with half the salt and the pepper. Bring 600ml (1 pint) of water to a simmer in a frying pan. Add the salmon, simmer for 2–3 minutes, cover tightly and turn off the heat. Let stand for 8 minutes.

Step two To make the sauce, combine the spring onions, ginger and remaining salt in a small bowl. In a small pan, combine the oils and heat to smoking point.

Step three Remove the salmon from the water and place on a plate. Scatter over the spring onion mixture, then pour over the hot oils and serve.

Peeled fresh root ginger can be stored in a glass jar, covered in rice wine or sherry, and sealed. It will keep for several months, and has the added benefit of producing a flavoured wine that can be used in cooking.

Malaysian Black Bean Fish

When I first tasted this dish during a visit to Malaysia, I immediately recognised the Chinese influence. However, it had a pungency that was uniquely Malay. Now I often make this tasty, light and satisfying dish, which is the hallmark of the best Malaysian home cooking.

Serves 4

450g (1lb) firm white fish fillets, such as cod, halibut, haddock or sea bass, skinned

3 tbsp groundnut oil

2 tsp salt

3 tbsp finely shredded spring onions, to garnish

for the sauce

1 tbsp groundnut oil

1½ tbsp coarsely chopped salted black beans

2 tbsp finely chopped garlic

2 tsp finely chopped fresh ginger

1 small onion, chopped

3 fresh green chillies, de-seeded and chopped

225g (8oz) button mushrooms, sliced

3 tbsp finely chopped spring onions

1 tbsp light soy sauce

1 tbsp lemon juice

1 tsp sugar

½ tsp salt

1 tsp freshly ground black pepper

Step one Cut the fish fillets into strips and set aside. Heat a wok or large frying pan over a high heat. Add the oil and, when it is very hot and slightly smoking, turn the heat down to medium and add the fish strips. Fry these gently for about 2 minutes or until they are brown on both sides, taking care not to break them up. Remove with a slotted spoon and drain on kitchen paper. Drain off most of the oil from the wok, leaving about 1½ tablespoons.

Step two Reheat the wok, add the groundnut oil for the sauce, plus the black beans, garlic, ginger and onion, and stir-fry for 2 minutes. Then add the chillies, button mushrooms and spring onions and stir-fry for another 3 minutes over a high heat.

Step three Now add the soy sauce, lemon juice, sugar, salt and pepper. Stir-fry for 10 seconds. Return the fish to the wok and gently finish cooking it in the sauce for about 1 minute. Give the mixture a good stir. Using a slotted spoon, arrange the fish on a warm serving platter, garnish with the spring onions and serve at once.

Fragrant Thai Meatballs

Walking through Bangkok, one is always pleasantly aware of exotic, mouth-watering aromas emanating from the many small restaurants and street stalls that line the thoroughfares. These meatballs are typical Thai street food. What makes them so deliciously savoury is the spices blending into the succulent beef and pork, while the egg white gives them a delicate, light texture. They are very easy to prepare and make.

Step one Process the beef and pork in a food-processor for a few seconds. Slowly add the egg white and cold water and process for a few more seconds, until fully incorporated into the meat. Add all the remaining ingredients except the flour and vegetable oil and process for about a minute, until the mixture becomes a light paste.

Step two Using your hands, shape the mixture into about 10 4cm (1½in) balls. Dust them evenly with flour, shaking off any excess. The meatballs will be quite fragile and soft.

Step three Heat a wok or large frying pan over a high heat. Add the oil and, when it is very hot and slightly smoking, gently drop in as many meatballs as will fit easily in one layer. Fry for about 4 minutes, adjusting the heat as necessary, until they are crisp and browned all over and cooked through. Remove with a slotted spoon and drain on kitchen paper, then repeat the process with any remaining meatballs. Serve at once.

Serves 4

100g (4oz) minced beef

100g (4oz) minced fatty pork

1 egg white

2 tbsp very cold water

1 tsp salt

½ tsp freshly ground black pepper

2 tbsp finely chopped garlic

3 tbsp finely chopped fresh coriander

2 tbsp finely chopped spring onions

1 tbsp fish sauce (nam pla)

2 tsp sugar

plain flour for dusting

450ml (15fl oz) vegetable oil for deep-frying

Cashew Chicken

This exemplifies the Chinese penchant for contrasting textures. Tender, succulent pieces of chicken are combined with sweet, crunchy cashew nuts. The secret to this popular dish is the use of that wonderful technique, velveting, in hot oil or water, which seals in the juices of the chicken, and then stir-frying as a second step to give it that special taste.

Serves 4

450g (1lb) boneless, skinless chicken breasts, cut into 1cm (½ in) chunks

1 egg white

1 tsp salt

1 tsp sesame oil

2 tsp cornflour

300ml (10fl oz) groundnut oil or water

2 tsp groundnut oil

50g (2oz) cashew nuts

1 tbsp Shaoxing rice wine or dry sherry

1 tbsp light soy sauce

1 tbsp finely shredded spring onions, to garnish

Step one Put the chicken in a bowl with the egg white, salt, sesame oil and cornflour and mix well. Chill for about 20 minutes.

Step two If you are using oil for velveting the chicken, heat a wok until very hot and then add the oil. When it is very hot, remove the wok from the heat and immediately add the chicken, stirring vigorously to prevent it sticking. After about 2 minutes, when the chicken turns white, quickly drain it and all of the oil in a colander set inside a bowl. Discard the oil. If you are using water, do exactly the same, but bring the water to the boil in a saucepan before adding the chicken. It will take about 4 minutes to turn white in the water.

Step three If you have used a wok, wipe it clean. Heat it until it is very hot, then add the 2 teaspoons of groundnut oil. Add the cashew nuts and stir-fry for 1 minute. Add the rice wine or sherry and soy sauce. Return the chicken to the wok and stir-fry for 2 minutes. Garnish with the spring onions and serve at once.

Sichuan-style Green Beans

This delectable dish originated in western China, as its seasonings indicate. The traditional recipe calls for Chinese asparagus or long beans, but I find green beans equally suitable. They are deep-fried to give them a soft, rather than a crunchy texture, but they should remain green and not be overcooked. After deep-frying, the beans are stir-fried in an array of spices. They should be slightly oily, but if they are too oily for your taste, you can blot them with kitchen paper before stir-frying them. For best results, serve the beans as soon as they are cooked. A delicious vegetarian dish.

Serves 4

600ml (1 pint) groundnut oil

450g (1lb) green beans, sliced if long; left whole otherwise

2 tbsp coarsely chopped garlic

1 tbsp finely chopped fresh root ginger

3 tbsp finely chopped spring onions (white part only)

1½ tbsp chilli bean sauce

1 tbsp whole yellow bean sauce

2 tbsp Shaoxing rice wine or dry sherry

1 tbsp dark soy sauce

2 tsp sugar

1 tbsp water

2 tsp chilli oil

Step one Heat a wok over a high heat. Add the oil and, when it is very hot and slightly smoking, deep-fry half the beans until slightly wrinkled, which should take about 3–4 minutes. Remove the beans and drain them on kitchen paper. Deep-fry the second batch in the same way.

Step two Transfer about 1 tablespoon of the oil in which you have cooked the beans to a clean wok or frying pan. Heat the oil, then add the garlic, ginger and spring onions and stir-fry for 30 seconds.

Step three Add all the rest of the ingredients except the green beans and stir-fry for 30 seconds.

Step four Add the drained beans and mix until they are thoroughly coated with the spicy mixture. Serve as soon as the beans have heated through.

Northern-style Cold Noodles

These savoury noodles are perfect for any meal or snack. They are quick and easy to make, but if you wish to prepare them ahead of time, keep the sauce and noodles separate until the last possible moment.

Serves 4

350g (12oz) dried or fresh egg noodles

2 tbsp sesame oil

3 tbsp finely chopped spring onions, to garnish

for the sauce

3 tbsp sesame paste or peanut butter

1½ tbsp finely chopped garlic

2 tsp finely chopped fresh root ginger

2 tsp chilli bean sauce

3 tbsp Chinese white vinegar or cider vinegar

2 tbsp orange juice

2 tbsp light soy sauce

2 tsp dark soy sauce

½ tsp salt

½ tsp freshly ground black pepper

2 tsp sugar

2 tsp ground roasted Sichuan peppercorns

1 tbsp groundnut oil

1½ tbsp sesame oil

Step one Cook the noodles in a large pan of boiling water for 3–5 minutes, then drain and plunge them in cold water. Drain the noodles thoroughly and toss them with the sesame oil. Arrange them on a platter or in a large bowl.

Step two To make the sauce, just mix all the ingredients together in a bowl or with an electric blender. It can be made in advance and kept refrigerated, as it is served cold. When ready to serve, pour the sauce on top of the noodles and toss well, then garnish with the spring onions.

Indonesian-style Sweetcorn Fritters

Here is an engaging dish – an enticing blend of sweetcorn and seasonings, all fried into crispy morsels. You can partially fry them beforehand and then plunge them into hot oil again just before serving.

Step one If using corn on the cob, remove the husks and silk and cut off the kernels with a sharp knife or cleaver. You should end up with about 275g (10oz) corn kernels. If you are using tinned corn, drain it thoroughly. In a blender or food-processor, combine half the corn with all the rest of the ingredients except the groundnut oil and fresh coriander. Blend to a purée, then pour into a bowl and mix in the rest of the corn. Let the mixture stand for at least 5 minutes.

Step two Heat a wok or deep saucepan over a high heat. Add the oil and, when it is very hot and slightly smoking, ladle a large spoonful of the sweetcorn mixture into it. Repeat until the wok is full. Reduce the heat to medium and cook the fritters for about 2 minutes, until golden brown underneath. Turn them over and fry the other side, then remove with a slotted spoon and drain on kitchen paper. Repeat with the remaining sweetcorn mixture. Arrange the fritters on a warm platter, garnish with the coriander and serve at once.

Serves 4–6

450g (1lb) corn on the cob, or 275g (10oz) tin of plain sweetcorn

5 shallots, finely sliced

2 tbsp finely chopped spring onions

2 tbsp finely chopped garlic

1 tsp ground coriander

½ tsp ground cumin

2 tsp salt

½ tsp freshly ground white pepper

1 tsp sugar

4 tbsp rice flour or plain flour

1 tsp baking powder

2 eggs, beaten

600ml (1 pint) groundnut oil, for deep-frying

2 tbsp finely chopped fresh coriander, or a few whole leaves, to garnish

Quick Pan-fried Five-spice Fish

The Chinese prefer to cook fish whole, although fish fillets and steaks can be satisfactorily used instead. We believe that the flesh remains moist and the flavour is best when the whole fish is used, head and tail included. To serve a fish whole is a symbol of prosperity. The head of the fish should always point in the direction of the guest of honour, a courtesy that assures him or her good fortune.

Serves 4

450g (1lb) fresh, firm white fish fillets, preferably cod or haddock

1 tsp five-spice powder

1 tsp salt

1½ tbsp groundnut oil

2 tbsp coarsely chopped garlic

2 tbsp coarsely chopped fresh root ginger

1½ tbsp Shaoxing rice wine or dry sherry

2 tsp light soy sauce

2 tsp sesame oil

rocket leaves, to garnish

Step one Rub the fish fillets with the five-spice powder and salt.

Step two Heat a wok or large frying pan until hot, then add the oil and reduce the heat. Gently pan-fry the fish on each side until lightly browned and remove from the wok with a spatula.

Step three Add the garlic, ginger, rice wine or sherry, soy sauce and sesame oil to the wok, then return the fish, gently reheat and serve, garnished with rocket.

Have you made this recipe? Tell us what you think at
www.mykitchentable.co.uk/blog

Northern Thai Chicken Noodle Soup

Khao soi is a wonderfully hearty but distinctly Thai soup, and quite delicious. A perfect dish for a large hungry crowd.

Serves 4–6

Step one Cook the noodles in a large pan of boiling water for 3–5 minutes, until tender. Drain thoroughly and set aside.

Step two Peel off the tough outer layers of the lemon grass, leaving the tender whitish centre. Cut it into 7.5cm (3in) pieces and crush with the flat of a heavy knife. Shred the chicken into strips.

Step three Heat a large, heavy pan over a high heat. Add the oil and, when it is very hot and slightly smoking, add the onion, garlic and lemon grass and stir-fry for about 3 minutes. Stir in the stock and coconut milk, reduce the heat to low, then cover and simmer for 10 minutes.

Step four Add the chillies, chicken, fish sauce, soy sauce, sugar, curry paste or powder, salt and pepper and stir well. Add the drained noodles, then cover and simmer for 5 minutes.

Step five Remove the lemon grass with a slotted spoon. Stir in the lime juice, then pour the soup into a large tureen, garnish with the coriander and basil leaves and serve at once.

175g (6oz) fresh or dried egg noodles

2 sticks of lemongrass

175g (6oz) boneless, skinless chicken breasts

1 tbsp vegetable oil

1 small onion, finely chopped

2 tbsp coarsely chopped garlic

1.2 litres (2 pints) home-made chicken stock (see page 7), vegetable stock or good-quality bought stock

1 x 400ml (14fl oz) tin of coconut milk

2 small, fresh red or green Thai chillies, de-seeded and finely shredded

1 tbsp fish sauce (nam pla)

1 tbsp dark soy sauce

1 tbsp sugar

2 tbsp Madras curry paste or powder

1 tsp salt

½ tsp freshly ground black pepper

2 tbsp lime juice

a handful of fresh coriander and basil leaves, to garnish

Spicy Prawn and Lemon Grass Soup

This delicious soup, called *tom yam ghoong*, is one of the most popular with Western fans of Thai food, combining spicy and sour in an enticing mixture of herbs and seasonings. It is not difficult to make and is a fine starting point for any meal.

Serves 4

2 sticks of lemon grass

1.2 litres (2 pints) home-made fish or chicken stock (see page 7) or good-quality bought stock

8 kaffir lime leaves, cut in half, or 1 tablespoon shredded lime zest

3 fresh red Thai chillies, de-seeded and finely shredded

¼ tsp black pepper

3 tbsp fish sauce (nam pla)

3 tbsp lime juice

225g (8oz) raw prawns, shelled and de-veined, tails on

2 spring onions (white and green parts), finely shredded

5 sprigs of coriander

Step one Peel off the tough outer layers of the lemon grass, leaving the tender whitish centre. Cut it into 7.5cm (3in) pieces and crush with the flat of a heavy knife.

Step two Bring the stock to a simmer in a large saucepan and add the lemon grass. Reduce the heat, then cover and simmer for 10 minutes. Remove the lemon grass with a slotted spoon and discard.

Step three Add the lime leaves or zest, chillies, black pepper, fish sauce and lime juice and simmer for 3 minutes. Now add the prawns, cover the pan and remove from the heat. Let stand for 10 minutes.

Step four Finally, stir in the spring onions and coriander. Ladle into a large soup tureen or individual bowls and serve immediately.

Singapore Classic Laksa

A one-dish meal of rice noodles, this is a fantastic dish to make for a crowd.

Step one Peel off the tough outer layers of the lemon grass, leaving the tender, whitish centre. Crush with the flat of a knife, then cut into 7.5cm (3in) pieces. De-seed and finely shred the chillies and finely slice the shallots.

Step two Heat a wok or large frying pan over a high heat. Add the oil and, when it is very hot and slightly smoking, add the lemon grass, garlic, ginger, chillies and shallots and stir-fry for 5 minutes.

Step three Now add the ground coriander, turmeric, salt and stock. Reduce the heat to low, cover and simmer for 20 minutes.

Step four Meanwhile, soak the rice noodles in a bowl of warm water for 20 minutes. Drain them in a colander or sieve. Add the coconut milk and rice noodles to the simmering stock. Season with the curry powder, shrimp paste, sugar and black pepper, add the prawns and continue to simmer for 10 minutes.

Step five While the dish is simmering, prepare the garnishes. Blanch the beansprouts in boiling water for 30 seconds, then drain and set aside. Hard-boil the eggs, allowing 4 minutes for quail's eggs and 8 minutes for hen's, then shell them. Cut the quail's eggs half and quarter the hen's eggs. Cut the lime or lemon into wedges.

Step six Ladle the laksa into a large soup tureen and serve at once, with the garnishes alongside.

Serves 4–6

2 sticks of lemon grass
2–3 fresh red chillies
225g (8oz) shallots
1½ tbsp groundnut oil,
2 tbsp chopped garlic
1 tbsp finely chopped fresh ginger
1 tsp ground coriander
½ tsp ground turmeric
1 tsp salt
1.2 litres (2 pints) home-made chicken stock (see page 7) or good-quality bought stock
225g (8oz) rice noodles or rice vermicelli
400ml (14fl oz) tinned coconut milk
2 tsp Madras curry powder
2 tsp shrimp paste
1 tsp sugar
½ tsp freshly ground black pepper
450g (1lb) raw prawns, shelled and de-veined

to garnish

3 tbsp finely sliced spring onions
200g (7oz) beansprouts
4 quail's or 2 hen's eggs
1 lime or lemon
sprigs of fresh coriander and mint

179

Peking-style Caramel Walnuts

This Peking-style treat is increasing in popularity throughout the West as more non-Cantonese recipes make their way on to Chinese restaurant menus. The shelled walnuts must be blanched first to rid them of any bitterness. Then they are rolled in sugar, left to dry for several hours and deep-fried to caramelise the sugar coating. Finally, they are rolled in sesame seeds. The result is a classic contrast of tastes and textures. They can be served hot or cold and are perfect with drinks.

Serves 4

225g (8oz) shelled
walnut halves

100g (4oz)
granulated sugar

450ml (15fl oz)
groundnut oil

3 tbsp sesame seeds

Step one Bring a large pan of water to the boil, add the walnut halves and then simmer for about 5 minutes. Drain through a colander or sieve.

Step two Pat the walnuts dry with kitchen paper and spread them on a baking tray. Sprinkle the sugar over the warm nuts and roll them in it to coat them completely. Place the tray in a cool, draughty place and leave to dry for at least 2 hours, preferably overnight. (They can be prepared ahead to this point.)

Step three Heat the oil to a moderate heat in a wok or deep-fat fryer. Fry a batch of the walnuts for about 2 minutes or until the sugar melts and the walnuts turn golden (adjust the heat if necessary to prevent burning). Remove the nuts from the oil.

Step four Sprinkle them with the sesame seeds and lay them on a wire rack to cool. (Do not drain them on kitchen paper or the sugar will stick when it dries.) Deep-fry and drain the rest of the walnuts in the same way. Serve warm or cold. Once cooled, the caramel walnuts can be kept in a sealed glass jar for about 2 weeks.

Sesame Prawn Toast

Sesame prawn toast is often served as an appetiser in Chinese restaurants. Its origins are rather obscure, but I suspect it is a variation on the prawn paste used widely in southern China as a stuffing or for deep-frying into crispy balls.

Step one Using a cleaver or sharp knife, chop the prawns coarsely and then mince them finely into a paste. Put them into a bowl and mix in the rest of the ingredients for the prawn paste. (Alternatively, you could do all this in a food-processor.) The paste can be made several hours in advance and kept, covered, in the fridge.

Step two Remove the crusts from the bread and cut it into rectangles about 7.5 x 2.5cm (3 x 1in) – you should have about 3 pieces per slice. If the bread is fresh, place it in a warm oven to dry out a little. Dry bread will absorb less oil.

Step three Spread the prawn paste thickly on each piece of bread. The paste should form a mound about 3mm (⅛in) deep, although you can spread it more thinly if you prefer. Sprinkle the toasts with the sesame seeds.

Step four Heat the oil to a moderate heat in a wok or deep-fat fryer. Deep-fry several prawn toasts at a time, paste-side down, for 2–3 minutes. Then turn them over and deep-fry for another 2 minutes, until they are golden brown. Remove with a slotted spoon, drain on kitchen paper and serve.

Makes about 30 pieces

10 thin slices
of white bread

3 tbsp white
sesame seeds

450ml (15fl oz)
groundnut oil

for the prawn paste

450g (1lb) raw prawns,
shelled and de-veined

100g (4oz) fresh
or tinned water
chestnuts, peeled if
fresh, finely chopped

100g (4oz)
minced fatty pork

1 tsp salt

½ tsp freshly ground
black pepper

1 egg white

3 tbsp finely chopped
spring onions (white
part only)

1½ tbsp finely
chopped fresh
root ginger

1 tbsp light soy sauce

2 tsp sesame oil

2 tsp sugar

Thai-style Spring Rolls

Although the Chinese influence is evident here, there is a Thai flavour in each bite – a pungent note not found in traditional Chinese spring rolls.

Makes about 30

5 tbsp plain flour

1 packet small, round rice paper wrappers

15fl oz (450ml) vegetable oil, for deep-frying

for the dipping sauce

2–3 small, fresh red Thai chillies, finely chopped

1 tbsp sugar

3 tbsp fish sauce (nam pla) or light soy sauce

3 tbsp lime juice

2 tsp water

for the filling

1½ tbsp vegetable oil

3 tbsp coarsely chopped garlic

175g (6oz) fresh crab meat

100g (4oz) minced pork

100g (4oz) raw prawns, shelled, de-veined and minced or finely chopped

2 tbsp fish sauce (nam pla)

1 tbsp light soy sauce

1 tsp sugar

½ tsp freshly ground black pepper

3 tbsp finely chopped fresh coriander

Step one In a small bowl, combine all the ingredients for the spicy dipping sauce. Set aside until ready to serve.

Step two Next, make the filling for the spring rolls. Heat a wok or large frying-pan over a high heat. Add the oil and, when it is very hot and slightly smoking, add the garlic and stir-fry for 30 seconds. Add the crab meat, pork, prawns, fish sauce, soy sauce, sugar and black pepper and stir-fry for 2 minutes. Remove from the heat and stir in the fresh coriander. Leave to cool completely.

Step three Put the flour in a small bowl, add 6 tablespoons of water and mix to a paste. Set aside.

Step four Fill a large bowl with warm water. Dip one of the rice paper rounds in the water and let it soften, then remove and drain on a tea towel. Put about a tablespoon of the filling on the softened rice paper wrapper. Fold in each side, roll up tightly and seal the ends with a little of the flour paste. You should have a roll about 5cm (2in) long, rather like a small sausage. Repeat with the remaining wrappers and filling. You may need to change the water occasionally as it cools.

Step five Heat the oil in a deep-fat fryer or large wok and deep-fry the spring rolls, a few at a time, for about 3 minutes, until golden brown and crisp. (Do not fry too many at once, as they have a tendency to stick together. If this happens, simply break them apart after they are cooked.) Drain on kitchen paper and serve at once with the dipping sauce.

Fish with Chilli Sauce

Freshwater fish of all sorts abound in the lakes and rivers of Thailand. They are usually prepared with pungent sauces, as in this *chuchi pla nuea orn*. But such sauces do not overwhelm their delicate flavour.

Step one Soak the dried chillies in warm water for about 5 minutes, until softened. Drain well and chop them finely.

Step two Heat a wok or large frying pan over a high heat. Add the oil and, when it is very hot and slightly smoking, stir in the chillies, garlic, shallots and shrimp paste. Stir-fry for 2 minutes, then add the fish sauce or soy sauce, sugar and water. Remove from the heat and pour the mixture into a bowl.

Step three Wipe the wok clean, add the oil for deep-frying and heat. Blot the trout dry inside and out with kitchen paper. Dust the outside thoroughly with flour, shaking off any excess.

Step four When the oil is very hot and slightly smoking, reduce the heat to medium and fry the trout for about 4 minutes on each side, until brown and crisp (you will probably have to do this in 2 batches). Remove the trout and drain on kitchen paper. Arrange on a platter, garnish with coriander sprigs and serve with the chilli sauce.

Serves 4

for the chilli sauce

5 dried red chillies

2 tbsp vegetable oil

100g (4oz) peeled garlic, finely chopped

100g (4oz) shallots, finely chopped

1 tbsp shrimp paste

2 tbsp fish sauce (nam pla) or light soy sauce

2 tsp sugar

4 tbsp water

for the fish

450ml (15fl oz) vegetable oil, for deep-frying

4 small trout, cleaned

plain flour, for dusting

sprigs of coriander, to garnish

Crispy Fish with Mango Salad

Pla samlee thod krob gub yam mamuang is a classic combination of flavours and textures. Fresh fish is fried until crisp, then served with a crunchy green mango salad. The results are sensational.

Serves 4

1 green, unripe mango

2–3 small, fresh red Thai chillies, de-seeded and shredded

2 tbsp finely sliced shallots

2 tbsp lime juice

1 tbsp fish sauce (nam pla)

1 tbsp sugar

1 x 900g (2lb) firm white fish, such as sea bass, cleaned or 450g (1lb) white fish fillet, cut into 4 pieces

plain flour, for dusting

450ml (15fl oz) vegetable oil, for deep-frying

3–4 tbsp crushed roasted peanuts, to garnish

Step one Peel the mango, then cut the flesh off the stone and shred finely.

Step two Mix the shredded mango with the chillies, shallots, lime juice, fish sauce and sugar. Set aside.

Step three If you are using a whole fish, score it by making 3 deep cuts on each side. Dry the fish or fish fillets on kitchen paper and dust with flour, shaking off any excess.

Step four Heat a wok or large frying pan over a high heat. Add the oil and, when it is very hot, add the fish and deep-fry until golden brown; this will take about 10–12 minutes for one large fish or about 5 minutes for fillets. Remove with a fish slice and drain immediately on kitchen paper. Garnish with the crushed peanuts and serve with the mango salad.

Whole Fish in Coconut Milk

In this traditional dish, called *pla tom gathi*, a whole fish is gently steamed to retain its succulence, subtle flavour and delicate texture. It is then paired with an aromatic coconut sauce. Simple steamed rice (see page 64) makes an ideal accompaniment. Instead of a whole fish you could use 450g (1lb) firm white fish fillets, in which case the cooking time should be reduced to about 5 minutes for flat fish such as sole, or 8–12 minutes for thicker ones such as cod.

Step one Peel off the tough outer layers of the lemon grass, leaving the tender whitish centre. Cut it into 7.5cm (3in) pieces and crush with the flat of a heavy knife.

Step two Put the lemon grass, galangal or ginger, lime leaves or zest, coriander roots, if using, and coconut milk in a pan and bring to the boil. Reduce the heat, then cover and simmer for 1 hour. Strain the liquid, discarding the lemon grass, galangal, lime leaves and coriander roots.

Step three Pat the fish dry on kitchen paper and score it on both sides by cutting slashes into the flesh.

Step four Set up a steamer or put a rack into a wok or deep pan and fill it with 5cm (2in) water. Bring to the boil over a high heat. Put the fish on a deep heatproof plate, pour the coconut mixture on top, then sprinkle over the shallots, fish sauce, lime juice and sugar. Put the plate of fish into the steamer or on the rack. Cover tightly and gently steam the fish for 15–20 minutes, until it is just cooked. Remove from the steamer, garnish with coriander leaves and serve at once.

Serves 4

2 sticks of lemon grass

2 tbsp coarsely chopped fresh galangal or fresh root ginger

6 kaffir lime leaves or 2 tbsp coarsely chopped lime zest

6 fresh coriander roots (optional)

1 x 400ml (14fl oz) tin of coconut milk

1 x 900g (2lb) fresh, firm white fish, such as sea bass, cod or halibut, cleaned

3 tbsp finely sliced shallots

3 tbsp fish sauce (nam pla)

2 tbsp lime juice

1 tbsp sugar

a handful of fresh coriander leaves, to garnish

Crackling Chinese Roast Pork

One of the most fascinating sights in Chinatowns all over the world is a shop with whole roast adult pigs as well as suckling pigs hanging in the window. The meat is delicious with rice or in stir-fried dishes. The secret of crispy skin is to blanch it and then let it dry using a technique similar to the one used for Peking Duck (see page 199). Then the skin is slowly roasted so that most of the fat runs off, leaving soft, tender pork flesh marbled with velvety fat. No wonder most diners are addicted to this delicious dish after the first bite. Much of the work can be done ahead of time and it is surprisingly easy.

Serves 4–6

1.5kg (3lb) boneless pork belly, with rind

Perfect Steamed Rice, to serve (optional, see page 64)

for the dry rub

2 tbsp coarse sea salt

1 tbsp ground roasted Sichuan peppercorns

2 tsp five-spice powder

1 tsp freshly ground black pepper

2 tsp sugar

Step one Pierce the rind side of the pork with a sharp fork or knife until the skin is covered with fine holes. Insert a meat hook into the pork.

Step two Bring a large pan of water to the boil. Hang the pork up from the meat hook and, using a large ladle, pour the hot water over the rind side several times. Set the pork aside.

Step three Heat a wok, then add all the ingredients for the dry rub and stir-fry for 3 minutes until they are well mixed. Leave to cool slightly. When the dry rub is cool enough to handle, rub it all over the flesh side of the pork.

Step four Hang the meat up to dry for 8 hours or overnight in a cool place or in front of a cold fan.

Step five Preheat the oven to 200°C/400°F/gas 6. Place the pork, rind-side up, on a rack over a roasting tin of water. Roast for 15 minutes, then reduce the heat to 180°C/350°F/gas 4 and continue to roast for 2 hours. Turn up the heat to 230°C/450°F/gas 8 and roast for a final 15 minutes. Remove the pork and leave to cool, then carve it into bite-sized pieces, arrange on a platter and serve. Alternatively, serve on beds of rice.

Five-spice Spareribs

These spareribs are marinated, deep-fried, then slowly braised in a piquant sauce.

Step one Separate the spareribs and cut them into 7.5cm (3in) chunks. Mix together the marinade ingredients and marinate the spareribs for 25 minutes at room temperature. Remove using a slotted spoon.

Step two Heat the oil in a deep-fat fryer or large wok until slightly smoking and slowly brown the spareribs, in batches, then drain on kitchen paper. (Leave the oil to cool and strain through a filter if you want to re-use when cooking pork.)

Step three Place the sauce ingredients in a clean wok or frying pan, bring to the boil, then reduce the heat. Add the spareribs, cover and gently simmer for 40 minutes, stirring occasionally. If necessary, add a little water to the sauce to prevent the spareribs from drying up. Skim off any surface fat and serve.

To make dried orange peel, peel the skin off an orange, scraping away as much of the white pith as possible or coarsely grate the peel. Lay on kitchen paper and dry in the sun, an airing cupboard or in a warm but turned off oven, until dry and very hard. Store in a tightly sealed container in a cool, dry place. To use, soak the required amount in warm water until it softens, then chop or slice according to the recipe. Add grated peel to dishes without soaking first.

Serves 4

750g pork spareribs
600ml (1 pint)
groundnut oil

for the marinade

1 tbsp Shaoxing rice wine or dry sherry

1 tbsp light soy sauce

1 tbsp Chinese black rice vinegar or cider vinegar

2 tsp sesame oil

1 tbsp cornflour

for the sauce

2 tbsp finely chopped garlic

2 tsp five-spice powder

3 tbsp finely chopped spring onions

3 tbsp Chinese rock sugar, white sugar or chunky amber sugar crystals

3 tbsp Shaoxing rice wine or dry sherry

150ml (¼ pint) home-made chicken stock (see page 7) or good-quality bought stock

1½ tbsp light soy sauce

2 tbsp dried grated orange peel (see tip)

85ml (3fl oz) Chinese black rice vinegar or cider vinegar

Spicy Chicken with Peanuts

This classic western Chinese dish is better known as *gongbao* or *kung pao* chicken. There are many versions of this recipe; this one is close to the original and is also easy to make.

Serves 4

3 tbsp groundnut oil

3 dried red chillies, halved lengthways

450g (1lb) boneless, skinless chicken breasts, cut into 2.5cm (1in) chunks

75g (3oz) roasted peanuts

for the sauce

2 tbsp home-made chicken stock (see page 7) or good-quality bought stock

2 tbsp Shaoxing rice wine or dry sherry

1 tbsp dark soy sauce

2 tsp sugar

1 tbsp coarsely chopped garlic

2 tsp finely chopped spring onions

1 tsp finely chopped fresh root ginger

2 tsp Chinese white rice vinegar or cider vinegar

1 tsp salt

2 tsp sesame oil

Step one Heat a wok over a high heat. Add the oil and chillies and stir-fry for a few seconds (you may remove the chillies when they turn black or leave them in).

Step two Add the chicken and peanuts and stir-fry for 1 minute. Remove the chicken, peanuts and chillies from the wok and drain in a colander.

Step three Put all the sauce ingredients, except the sesame oil, into the wok. Bring to the boil and then reduce the heat.

Step four Return the chicken, peanuts and chillies to the wok and cook for about 3–4 minutes in the sauce, mixing well. Finally, add the sesame oil, give the mixture a good stir, remove the chillies, if you prefer, and serve straight away.

Peking Duck

Preparing Peking Duck is a time-consuming task, but I have devised a simpler method that gives impressive results, closely approximating the real thing. Each guest spoons some sauce on to a pancake, then places a helping of crisp skin and meat on top with some spring onion shreds and cucumber sticks. The entire mixture is rolled up in the pancake and then eaten using chopsticks or one's fingers.

Step one If the duck is frozen, thaw it thoroughly. Rinse it well and blot completely dry with kitchen paper. Insert a meat hook near the neck. Combine the ingredients for the honey syrup in a large wok or pan and bring to the boil. Holding the duck up by the meat hook, use a large ladle or spoon to pour the syrup over the duck several times, as if to bathe it, until the skin is completely coated with the mixture. Once used, the mixture can be discarded.

Step two Hang the duck to dry in a cool, well-ventilated place, or hang it in front of a cold fan for about 4–5 hours, longer if possible. Be sure to put a tray or roasting tin underneath to catch any drips. Once the duck has dried, the skin will feel like parchment.

Step three Preheat the oven to 240°C/475°F/gas 9. Place the duck, breast-side up, on a roasting rack in a roasting tin. Put 150ml (5fl oz) of water into the tin (this will prevent the fat splattering). Now put the duck into the oven and roast it for 15 minutes. Reduce the heat to 180°C/350°F/gas 4 and continue to roast for 1 hour 10 minutes. Replenish the water as necessary.

Step four Remove the duck from the oven and let it sit for at least 10 minutes before you carve it. Using a cleaver or a sharp knife, cut the skin and meat into pieces and arrange them on a warm platter. Serve at once, with the Chinese Pancakes, spring onions, cucumber and a bowl of hoisin sauce or sweet bean sauce for guests to help themselves.

Serves 4–6

1 x 2.75kg (6lb)
duck, fresh or
frozen, preferably
Cherry Valley

for the honey syrup

2 tbsp cider vinegar

1.2 litres
(2 pints) water

3 tbsp honey

3 tbsp dark soy sauce

to serve

Chinese Pancakes
(see page 203)

4 spring onions,
finely shredded

1 cucumber, peeled,
de-seeded and cut
into 5 x 2.5cm
(2 x 1in) pieces

6 tbsp hoisin sauce or
sweet bean sauce

199

Crispy Aromatic Duck

This is probably one of the best-selling dishes in Chinese restaurants in the West. Although it is available as a ready-cooked meal, nothing beats the home-made version. Don't be intimidated by the long preparation process. Most of the steps are quite straightforward and can be done up to a day ahead, and the results are well worth the labour.

Serves 4–6

1 x 2.75kg (6lb) duck, fresh or frozen, preferably Cherry Valley

6 slices of fresh root ginger, 7.5cm x 5mm (3 x ¼in)

6 spring onions, cut into 7.5cm (3in) lengths

cornflour, plain flour or potato flour for dusting

1.2 litres (2 pints) groundnut oil

for the spice rub

2 tbsp five-spice powder

65g (2½ oz) Sichuan peppercorns

25g (1oz) whole black peppercorns

3 tbsp cumin seeds

200g (7oz) rock salt

to serve

Chinese Pancakes (see page 203)

6 spring onions, finely shredded

hoisin sauce

Step one If the duck is frozen, thaw it thoroughly. Rinse well and blot it completely dry with kitchen paper. Mix all the ingredients for the spice rub together in a small bowl, then rub the duck inside and out with this mixture, applying it evenly. Wrap well in clingfilm and place in the fridge for 24 hours.

Step two After this time, brush any excess spices from the duck. Stuff the ginger and spring onions into the cavity and put the duck on a heatproof plate. Set up a steamer or put a rack into a wok. Fill it with 5cm (2in) of water and bring to the boil. Lower the duck and plate into the steamer and cover tightly. Steam gently for 2 hours, pouring off excess fat from time to time. Add more water as necessary. Remove the duck from the steamer and pour off all the liquid. Discard the ginger and spring onions. Leave the duck in a cool place for 2 hours or until it has dried and cooled. At this point the duck can be refrigerated.

Step three Just before you are ready to serve it, cut the duck into quarters and dust with cornflour, plain flour or potato flour, shaking off the excess.

Step four Heat the oil in a wok or deep-fat fryer. When it is almost smoking, deep-fry the duck quarters in 2 batches. Fry the breasts for about 8–10 minutes and the thighs and legs for about 12–15 minutes, until each quarter is crisp and heated right through. Drain the duck on kitchen paper and leave until cool enough to handle. Then remove the meat from the bones and shred it. You can do this easily with a fork. The Chinese eat it with bones and all. Serve with the Chinese Pancakes, spring onions and hoisin sauce.

Chinese Pancakes

These pancakes are the classic accompaniment to Peking Duck (see page 199) and Crispy Aromatic Duck (see page 200) and reflect the northern Chinese use of wheat instead of rice. They are easy to make once you get the knack, which comes with practice.

Serves 6–8

275g (10oz) plain flour, plus extra for dusting

250ml (8fl oz) very hot water

2 tbsp sesame oil

Step one Put the flour into a large bowl. Gradually stir in the hot water, mixing all the while with chopsticks or a fork until it is fully incorporated. Add more water if the mixture seems dry.

Step two Turn the dough out and knead it with your hands for about 8 minutes or until it is smooth, dusting with flour if necessary, as it may be quite sticky at this point. Put the dough back into the bowl, cover it with a damp tea towel and let it rest for about 30 minutes.

Step three Remove the dough from the bowl and knead again for about 5 minutes, dusting with a little flour if it is sticky. Once the dough is smooth, form it into a roll about 45cm (18in) long and 2.5cm (1in) thick. Cut the roll into 18 equal pieces and shape each one into a ball.

Step four Take 2 of the dough balls. Dip one side of one ball into the sesame oil and place the oiled side on top of the other ball. With a rolling pin, roll the 2 pancakes simultaneously into a circle about 15cm (6in) in diameter. You can flip the double pancake over and roll on the other side as well.

Step five Heat a frying pan or wok over a very low heat. Put the double pancake into the pan and cook it for 1–2 minutes, until it has dried underneath; there may be brown specks. Flip it over and cook the other side until dried as well. Remove from the pan and leave to cool slightly. When it is still warm, but cool enough to handle, peel the 2 pancakes apart and set them aside. Repeat this process until all the dough balls have been cooked.

Sweet and Sour Aubergines

This easy dish, called *yam makhua*, makes a delectable accompaniment to any meal. If you substitute light soy sauce for the fish sauce it will be quite suitable for vegetarians.

Serves 2–4

450g (1lb) aubergines

3 tbsp finely
sliced shallots

2 tbsp fish sauce (nam
pla) or light soy sauce

2 tbsp lime juice

1 tbsp sugar

a handful of fresh
coriander leaves,
to garnish

Step one Preheat the oven to 240°C/475°F/gas 9. Using a sharp knife, prick the skin of the aubergines. Place them in a roasting tin and bake for 30–40 minutes, until they are soft. Leave to cool.

Step two Peel the aubergines, then put them in a colander and leave to drain for at least 30 minutes. Dice them and place in a bowl (this can all be done several hours in advance).

Step three Put the shallots, fish sauce or soy sauce, lime juice and sugar in a saucepan and bring to a simmer. Pour this mixture over the aubergines and mix well. Garnish with the coriander leaves and serve.

**KITCHEN
TABLE**

For a video masterclass on knife skills, go to
www.mykitchentable.co.uk/videos/knifeskills

10 9 8 7 6 5 4 3 2 1

Published in 2012 by BBC Books, an imprint of Ebury
Publishing. A Random House Group company.

Recipes © Promo Group Ltd 2012
Book design © Woodlands Books Ltd 2012

All recipes contained in this book first appeared in Ken Hom's
Hot Wok (1996), Foolproof Chinese Cookery (2000), Foolproof
Thai Cookery (2002) and Foolproof Asian Cookery (2003).

Ken Hom has asserted his right to be identified as the author
of this Work in accordance with the Copyright, Designs and
Patents Act 1988

The Random House Group Limited
Reg. No. 954009

A CIP catalogue record for this book is available from the
British Library

The Random House Group Limited supports The Forest
Stewardship Council (FSC®), the leading international
forest certification organisation. Our books carrying the
FSC label are printed on FSC® certified paper. FSC is the
only forest certification scheme endorsed by the leading
environmental organisations, including Greenpeace. Our
paper procurement policy can be found at
www.randomhouse.co.uk/environment

Addresses for companies within the Random House Group
can be found at www.randomhouse.co.uk

To buy books by your favourite authors and register for offers
visit www.randomhouse.co.uk

Printed and bound in the UK by Butler, Tanner and
Dennis Ltd
Colour origination by AltaImage

Commissioning Editor: Muna Reyal
Project Editor: Joe Cottington
Designer: Lucy Stephens
Photographer: William Reavell © Woodlands Books
Ltd 2012 (see also credits below)
Food Stylists: Sarah Ramsbottom, Linda Tubby, Marie-Ange
Lapierre, Penny Stephens, Julia Azzarello and Mari Williams
Prop stylist: Sue Rowlands
Copy Editor: Anne Newman
Production: Rebecca Jones

Photography on p4 Noel Murphy © Woodlands Books Ltd
2010; pages 57, 58, 61, 62, 85, 98, 158 and 173 Philip Webb ©
Woodlands Books Ltd 1996; pages 6, 9, 10, 13, 14, 17, 18, 21,
22, 25, 26, 29, 30, 33, 34, 37, 38, 41, 42, 45, 46, 49, 50, 53, 54,
65, 66, 69, 70, 73, 74, 77, 78, 81, 82, 141, 142, 145, 146, 149,
150, 153, 154, 157, 161, 162, 165, 166, 169, 170, 174, 177, 178,
181, 182, 185, 186, 189, 190, 193, 197, 198, 201, 202 and 205
© Jean Cazals 2000, 2002 and 2003.

ISBN: 9781849903981